MW00651554

WILFRID
LUPANO

LÉONARD
CHEMINEAU

The Library Mule of Córdoba

COLORS:
CHRISTOPHE BOUCHARD

TRANSLATION & LETTERING:
LYNN ESKOW WITH RODOLFO MURAGUCHI

I dedicate this book to Eneko and Oscar who came with me to walk
in the mountains with a mule to see what it's like.

I would like to thank Valérie Beniest, Cécile Frappé, Yves Schlirf, Murielle Briot, and the entire Dargaud team for their incredible commitment to this book for nearly five years.
Thanks to Clotilde for her keen eye. Thanks to Chafika for her advice.
Thanks to Pascal Buresi for agreeing to help us steer this darn mule a bit.
Finally, thanks to Léonard Chemineau for not being afraid of the mountain of work that was the journey of The Library Mule of Cordoba. Thank you for your creativity, your unwavering determination, and your good humor. Let's do it again whenever you want.

WILFRID LUPANO

First and foremost, I thank Ferdinand, who proposed multiple sketches for the cover and created the drawings of Tarid as a young man (page 78).

Thanks to Valérie Beniest, Yves Schlirf, and the entire Dargaud team for their trust from the start and throughout the creation.
Thanks to Monique Buresi for her invaluable help in finding Arabic calligraphy dating back to the 10th centu

And finally, a huge thank you to Wilfrid Lupano for offering me this extraordinary project. I have always wanted to make books to change the world and grow within myself. Well, you see, I have the feeling that our good old mule has contributed on both counts.

LÉONARD CHEMINEAU

We would like to thank for their precious help on the colors:
Bruno Tatti, Clémence Sapin, Delf, Gabrielle Penager, Eve Gros,
Calvin Kim, Hayden Kerspern, Luan Kodra, Kevan Goy

Graphic design and artistic direction:
Philippe Ravon

Calligraphy of pages 9, 78, 90, 130 and 255:
Ségolène Ferté

FOR ABLAZE

Managing Editor **Rich Young** | Editor **Kevin Ketner** | Associate Editor **Amy Jackson**
Designers **Rodolfo Muraguchi** & **Julia Stezovsky**

Publisher's Cataloging-in-Publication data

Names: Lupano, Wilfrid, author. | Chemineau, Léonard, artist.
Title: The library mule of Córdoba / written by Wilfrid Lupano; art by Léonard Chemineau.
Description: Portland, OR: Ablaze, 2024.
Identifiers: ISBN: 978-1-68497-279-1
Subjects: LCSH Córdoba (Spain)—History—To 1500—Comic books, strips, etc. | Córdoba (Spain)—History—To 1500—Fiction. | Cities and towns, Medieval—Spain—Comic books, strips, etc. | Cities and towns, Medieval—Spain—Fiction. | Librarians—Comic books, strips, etc. | Librarians—Fiction. | Mules—Comic books, strips, etc. | Mules—Fiction. | Graphic novels. | BISAC COMICS & GRAPHIC NOVELS / Historical Fiction / Medieval | COMICS & GRAPHIC NOVELS / Humorous
Classification: LCC PS3612 .U73 L53 2024 | DDC 741.5—dc23

THE LIBRARY MULE OF CÓRDOBA. Published by Ablaze Publishing, 11222 SE Main St. #22906 Portland, OR 97269.

10 9 8 7 6 5 4 3 2 1

Córdoba, end of the 10th Century.

Surviving descendants of the Umayyad Dynasty have established the Emirate of Al-Andalus as a Caliphate. They aspire to compete with Baghdad, where the Abbasids, who massacred their ancestors, reign.

Two Umayyad rulers in particular, the Caliphs Abd al-Rahman III and his son, Al-Hakam II, devoted their lives to making their capital of Córdoba the center of all knowledge and artistic pursuit. They built public universities, collected thousands of works, welcomed scholars, and developed the art of copying texts in Arabic, all in an effort to promote Córdoba as the largest cultural center in the West of the Known World.

But, in 976, Al-Hakam II died suddenly following a stroke. His young son and heir, Hisham, was only eleven years old...

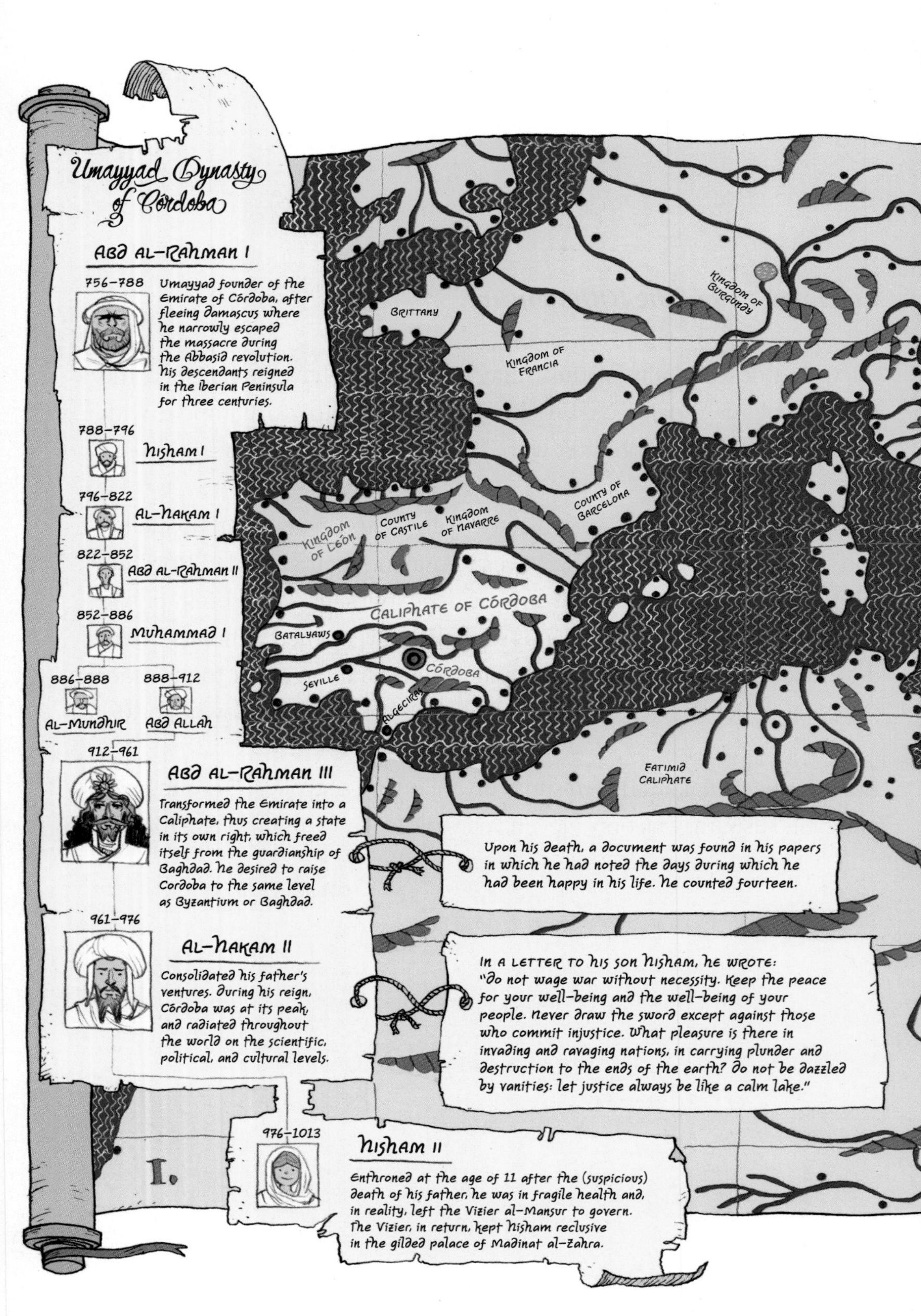
Umayyad Dynasty of Córdoba
Abd al-Rahman I
756–788
Umayyad founder of the Emirate of Córdoba, after fleeing Damascus where he narrowly escaped the massacre during the Abbasid revolution. His descendants reigned in the Iberian Peninsula for three centuries.
788–796
Hisham I
796–822
Al-Hakam I
822–852
Abd al-Rahman II
852–886
Muhammad I
886–888
Al-Mundhir
888–912
Abd Allah
912–961
Abd al-Rahman III
Transformed the Emirate into a Caliphate, thus creating a state in its own right, which freed itself from the guardianship of Baghdad. He desired to raise Cordoba to the same level as Byzantium or Baghdad.
Upon his death, a document was found in his papers in which he had noted the days during which he had been happy in his life. He counted fourteen.
961–976
Al-Hakam II
Consolidated his father's ventures. During his reign, Córdoba was at its peak, and radiated throughout the world on the scientific, political, and cultural levels.
In a letter to his son Hisham, he wrote: "Do not wage war without necessity. Keep the peace for your well-being and the well-being of your people. Never draw the sword except against those who commit injustice. What pleasure is there in invading and ravaging nations, in carrying plunder and destruction to the ends of the earth? Do not be dazzled by vanities: let justice always be like a calm lake."
976–1013
Hisham II
Enthroned at the age of 11 after the (suspicious) death of his father, he was in fragile health and, in reality, left the Vizier al-Mansur to govern. The Vizier, in return, kept Hisham reclusive in the gilded palace of Madinat al-Zahra.
Brittany
Kingdom of Burgundy
Kingdom of Francia
County of Barcelona
Kingdom of León
County of Castile
Kingdom of Navarre
Caliphate of Córdoba
Batalyaws
Córdoba
Seville
Algeciras
Fatimid Caliphate
I.

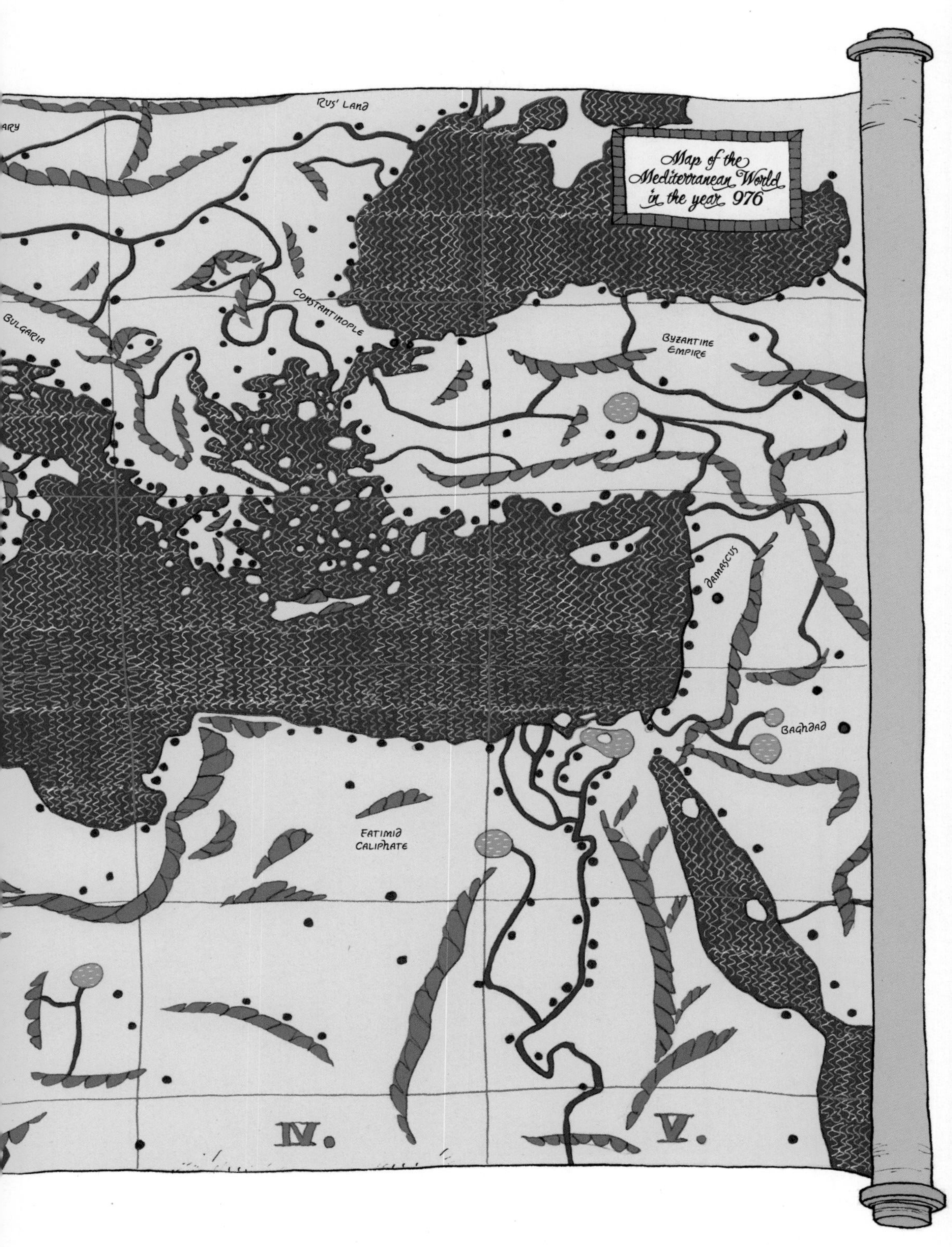
Map of the Mediterranean World in the year 976
Rus' Land
Constantinople
Bulgaria
Byzantine Empire
Damascus
Baghdad
Fatimid Caliphate
IV.
V.

HUFF!
HUFF!
HUFF!
HUFF!

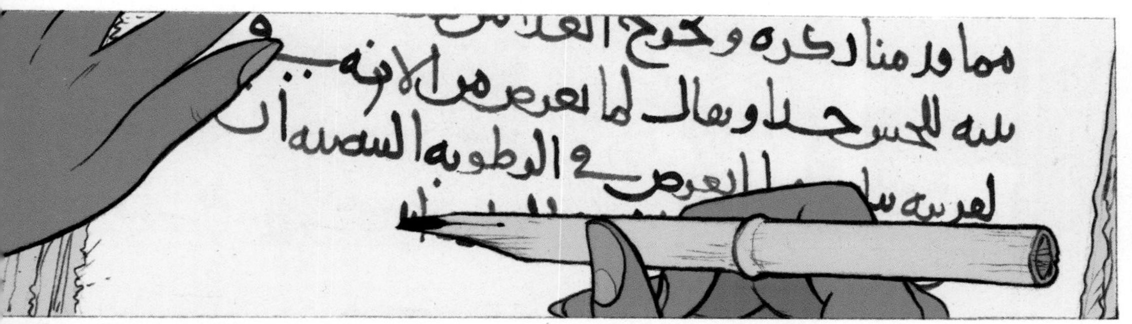

HUFF!
HUFF!

LUBNA!
THEY...
THEY...

WHAT'S GOING ON, TARID?
THEY'RE GOING THROUGH WITH IT! TOMORROW!
YOU...
SO, YOU WERE RIGHT. HOW HORRIBLE.

WELCOME TO CÓRDOBA, YOU POOR OLD FOOL!
THIS IS WHERE YOU AND I PART WAYS!
THIS IS WHERE I'M SELLING YOU, NO MATTER THE OFFER!
WHOEVER BUYS YOU CAN DO WHATEVER THEY WISH WITH YOU!
THEY CAN COOK YOU INTO A STEW, FOR ALL I CARE! SO LONG AS I NEVER HAVE TO SEE YOU AGAIN!
YOU'RE THE WORST MULE I'VE EVER MET IN MY ENTIRE LIFE!

AND YOU'RE ALSO THE LAST.
BECAUSE... NOW THAT THE CALIPH AL-HAKAM II IS DEAD, REST HIS SOUL, AND HIS YOUNG SON, HISHAM, IS ONLY ELEVEN YEARS OLD... WHO'S THE GREATEST POWER IN THE CALIPHATE OF CÓRDOBA?
VIZIER MUHAMMAD AMIR!
I'M A PERSONAL FRIEND OF THE GRAND VIZIER!
MY CHILDHOOD FRIEND! HAHAHA! CAN YOU IMAGINE MY LUCK?
MY LIFE'S ABOUT TO CHANGE!
AND I SWEAR TO YOU: IN THE FUTURE, YOU'LL NEVER SEE ME RIDE A MULE AGAIN!
I'M GOING TO BECOME SOMEONE IMPORTANT, AND I'LL ONLY RIDE SUPERB HORSES.
BUT FIRST, THERE IS A MISTAKE I MUST CORRECT.
PAT
PAT

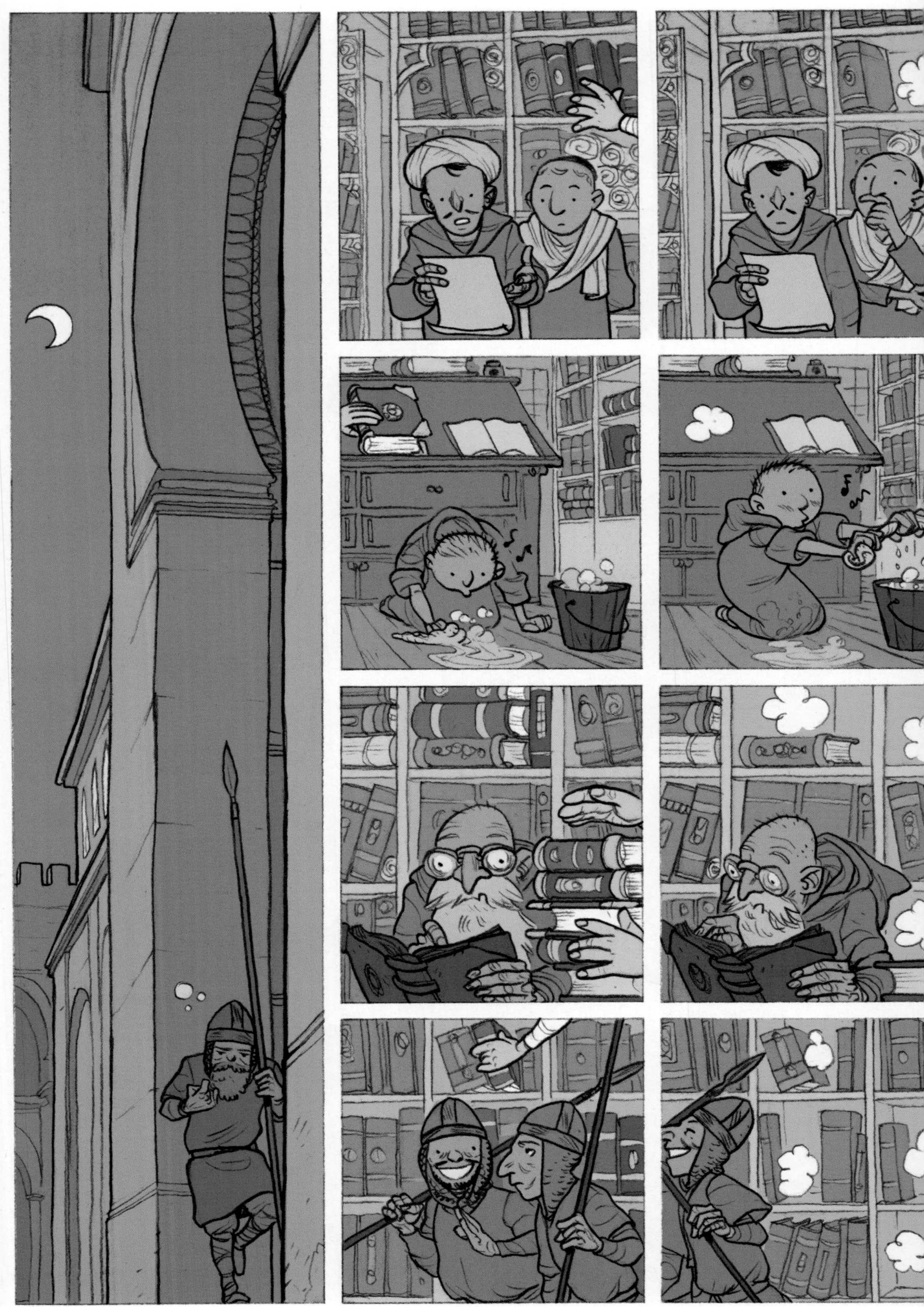

CLAC

TARID, THIS IS TOO MUCH!
WE CAN'T MOVE ALL OF THIS!
WE MUST!

AND HOW DO YOU PROPOSE WE DO IT?
I FOUND THIS ROPE. I'M GOING TO BRING EVERYTHING DOWN TO THE GARDEN, AND THEN...

...AND THEN

I'LL GO DOWN TO RECEIVE THE BOOKS.
NO! I CAN MANAGE!

YOU WON'T BE ABLE TO DO IT ALONE.
LET ME HELP YOU.

IT'S LATE. I'M GOING HOME. GOOD NIGHT.
G'NIGHT.

HALT! THE ALCÁZAR AND ITS GARDENS ARE CLOSED AT THIS TIME.

I'M HERE TO VISIT MY FORMER MASTER, THE LIBRARIAN TARID.

IT'S A SURPRISE.

I HAVEN'T SEEN HIM IN TEN YEARS.
HEM HEM...
CLING

OKAY, BUT BE QUICK.

HEHEH! THAT'S WHERE I USED TO HIDE WITH THE OTHER DISCIPLES.
I WONDER IF I CAN STILL CLIMB UP THERE.

WHAT...?!

THIEVES.

THEY'RE OUT OF LUCK. I'M ARMED FOR ONCE!

HEY!
STOP RIGHT THERE!

ES?

UH...
G... GOOD EVENING... I...

HUUUUUUN!

OUYOUYOUYOU YA

BUMF

?!
WHAT WAS THAT NOISE? IS THERE A PROBLEM?

NO. GOOD NEWS, ACTUALLY. I FOUND A MULE.

A MULE! I'LL GO FIND A FEW MORE BOOKS, THEN!
NO! WE CAN'T--

RAAAH!

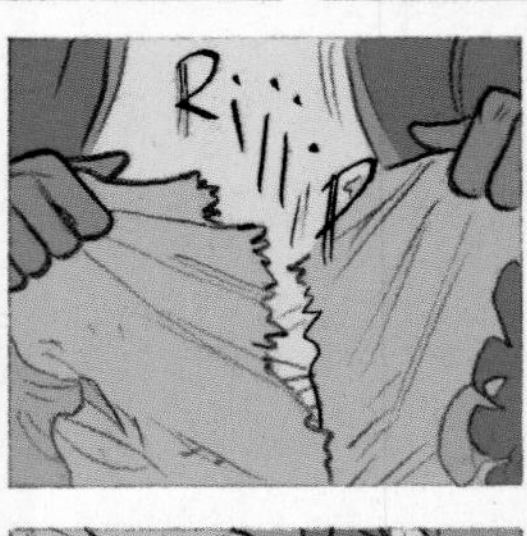
RIIIIP

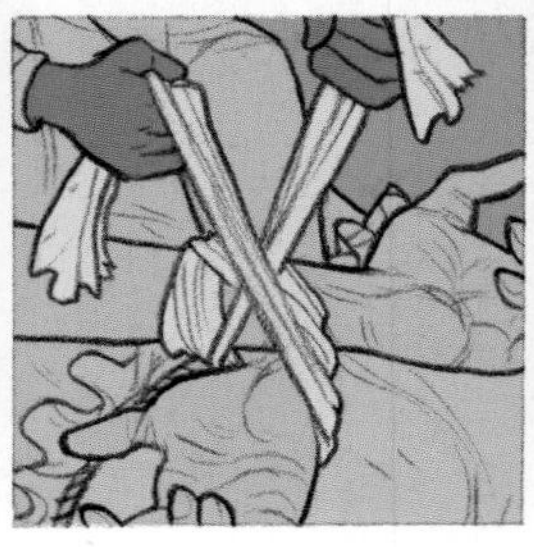

IT'S TOO MUCH...

... WAY TOO MUCH FOR THIS POOR BEAST.
WE DON'T HAVE A CHOICE.

BUNK
YOU SHOULD TAKE IT EASIER ON THE BOOKS...
LET'S GO!

COME ON! WHAT'S WRONG WITH YOU?!
SHE'S TOO BURDENED! YOU TOOK TOO MANY BOOKS!
HOW CAN YOU SAY THAT?! I SHOULD HAVE TAKEN TEN TIMES MORE! A HUNDRED TIMES MORE!
SHHHH...!

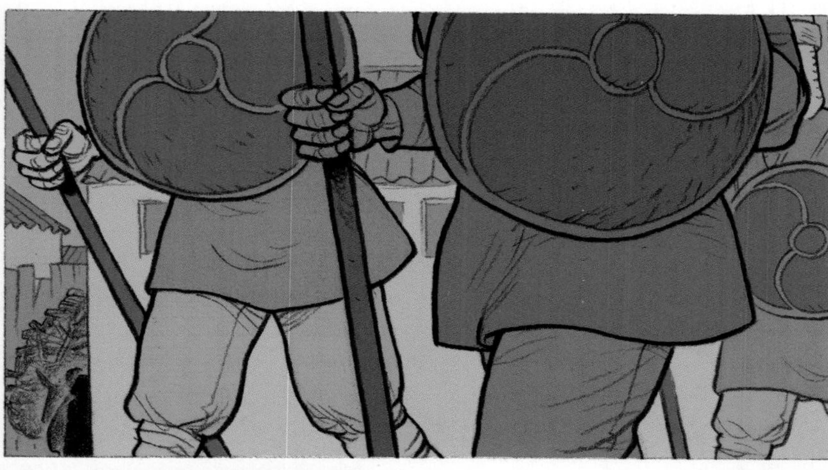

GO HOME NOW. YOU'VE ALREADY RISKED TOO MUCH.
I WANT TO GO WITH YOU.
OUT OF THE QUESTION!
YOU KNOW WHAT CAN HAPPEN TO RUNAWAY SLAVES!

IF WE'RE CAUGHT, WE'LL SURELY BE PUT TO DEATH! YOU'RE YOUNG! YOU HAVE A LIFE TO LIVE!
LEAVE! GO! EVERYTHING WILL BE FINE! GO HOME!
ALRIGHT. IF YOU NEED IT, YOU HAVE A SWORD HERE. IT BELONGED TO THE MAN I KNOCKED OUT.

A SWORD? WHAT DO YOU WANT ME TO DO WITH A SWORD? HAVE YOU SEEN ME?

I'LL NEVER FORGET YOU, TARID.
THANK YOU FOR EVERYTHING. FAREWELL.

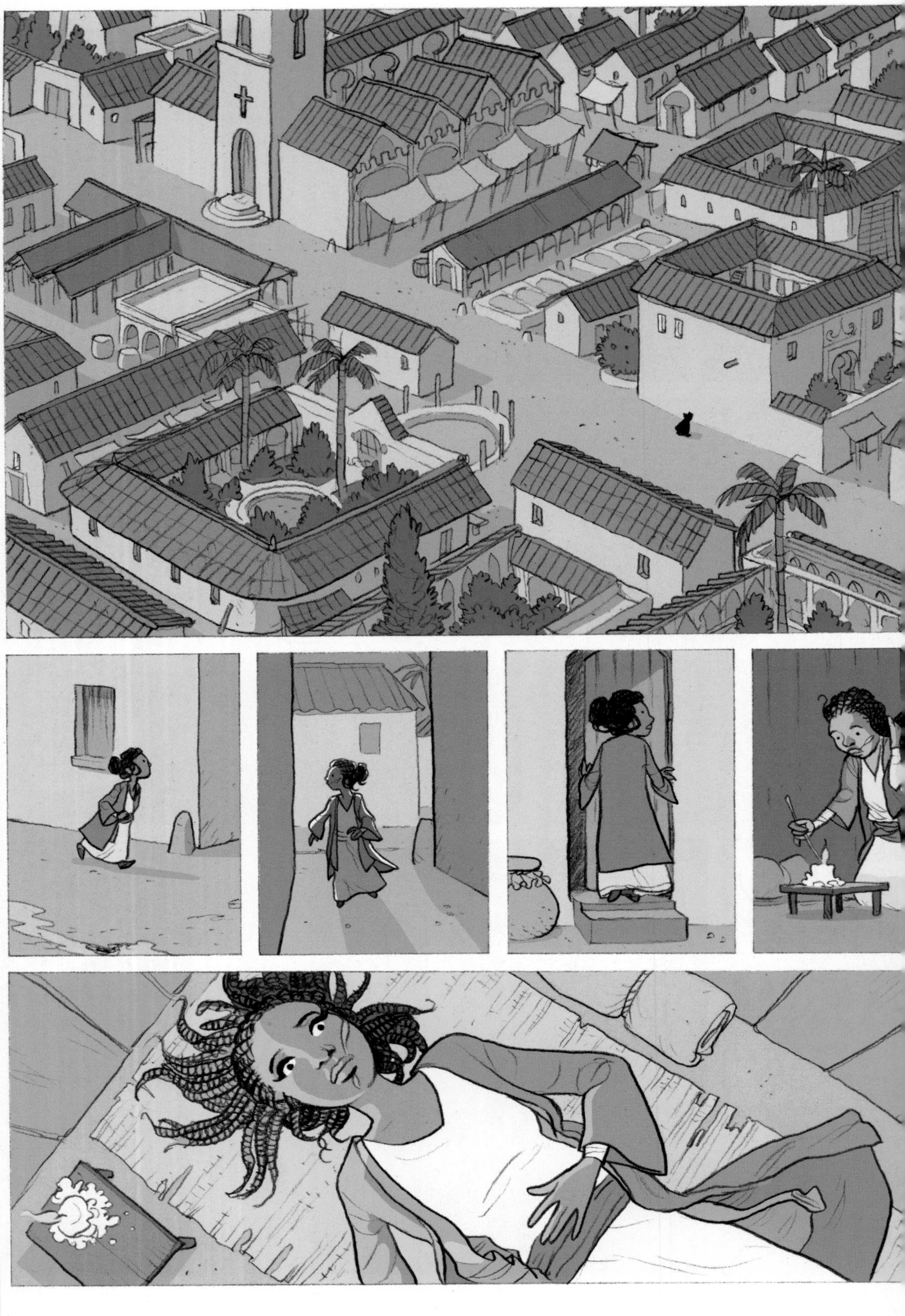

POF
PLAF
PAF
BOM
PAF
WHAT ARE YOU DOING HERE?

THAT'S HIM, SIR.
YOU WERE AN ACCOMPLICE HERE, IS THAT RIGHT?
AN ACCOMPLICE?! WHOSE?!
TARID, THE LIBRARIAN. YOU KNOW TARID?
HE TOLD ME HE KNEW HIM, SIR.
YEAH, I KNOW HIM. I WAS HIS APPRENTICE TEN YEARS AGO, BUT...
HE STOLE BOOKS. LOTS OF BOOKS. BUT YOU ALREADY KNOW THAT, DON'T YOU?
WHAT? TARID?!?

IMPOSSIBLE! HE'S THE MOST HONEST MAN IN THE WORLD!
WELL, WE'RE SURE OF IT. AND NOW HE'S DISAPPEARED.

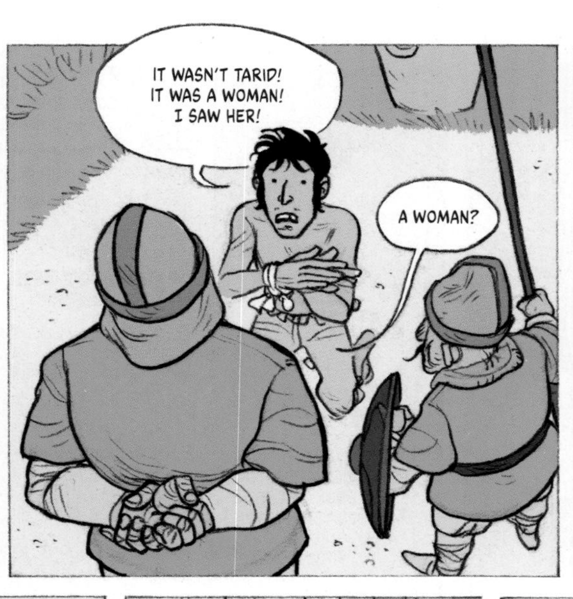
IT WASN'T TARID! IT WAS A WOMAN! I SAW HER!
A WOMAN?

VERY BEAUTIFUL, WITH DARK SKIN... BUT SHE HAD A SCAR.

O WOMEN IN THE LIBRARY LAST GHT, SIR. THE GUARD TOLD ME HAT THE LAST COPYIST, LUBNA, RETURNED HOME BEFORE THE CIDENT. ONLY TARID REMAINED.
AND WHAT IS THIS LUBNA LIKE?

SHE HAS DARK SKIN... AND A SCAR.
SEE?! IT'S HER! AND IT'S NOT ME!
PLAF

IT'S TARID MOST OF ALL! AND I THINK YOU HELPED HIM.
FIND ME THIS COPYIST. I WANT TO QUESTION HER.

S FOR YOU, CAN YOU WEAR TO GOD THAT OU HAVEN'T STOLEN NY BOOKS FROM THE CALIPH'S LIBRARY?
WELL... GULP! I... UH... YEAH, UM...

THAT'S NOT VERY CONVINCING.
THAT IS TO SAY... I DID TAKE A BOOK, BUT THAT WAS TEN YEARS AGO!

WHAT?

I WAS ONLY A CHILD! AN APPRENTICE!
I RAN AWAY WITH A RARE BOOK IN ORDER TO SELL IT! AND I JUST CAME BACK TO RETURN IT!

AND WHY WOULD YOU RETURN A BOOK YOU STOLE TEN YEARS AGO?

TO OBTAIN GOD'S FORGIVENESS, OF COURSE!
AND... TARID'S, AS WELL. HE'S THE ONE WHO TAUGHT ME THE VALUE OF HONESTY!
HMM. BUT YOU STILL TOOK THE BOOK FROM HIM.

THAT'S JUST BECAUSE IT TOOK ME A LONG TIME TO UNDERSTAND HIS TEACHINGS.

HMM. AND WHERE IS THIS BOOK?
WITH MY MULE!

HE DID HAVE A MULE, SIR.
AND WHERE THIS MULE?

I DON'T KNOW!

NO MULES TO BE SEEN, SIR.
NO BOOKS AND NO MULES.

GOOD. SO TARID, THE LIBRARIAN, STOLE SOME BOOKS...
...AND YOU, HO HAPPENS TO BE FORMER APPRENTICE AN ADMITTED BOOK IEF, HAVE COME TO ETURN A STOLEN BOOK.
YES.
SPECIFICALLY TO THE MAN WHO JUST STOLE SEVERAL BOOKS.
YES.

SPECIFICALLY TODAY?
YES.

ALL THIS, AND NOW YOUR MULE'S JUST DISAPPEARED.
YES.

HE'S MAKING FUN OF YOU, SIR.
I NOTICED. CUT OFF HIS HEAD.

WHAT?!?
WAIT! YOU CAN'T DO THAT!
I...
I'M A PERSONAL FRIEND OF VIZIER MUHAMMAD AMIR!

HAHAHA HA HAHA

IT'S TRUE! I WAS HIS COURIER AS A CHILD!
IT'S EVEN THANKS TO HIM THAT I WAS ABLE TO BECOME AN APPRENTICE AT THE GREAT LIBRARY!
ASK HIM! WE WERE INSEPARABLE!
ARE YOU INSINUATING THAT GRAND VIZIER AMIR IS FRIENDS WITH THIEVES?!
THAT IT WAS **HE** WHO ALLOWED A THIEF LIKE YOU ACCESS TO THE GREAT LIBRARY TO STEAL ITS PRECIOUS WORKS?!
EUH... HEHE...
ARE WE STILL CUTTING HIS HEAD OFF, SIR?
NO.
AH!
THROW HIM IN THE RIVER. HIS DEATH WILL BE SLOWER.

YOU'RE ABOUT TO COMMIT A GREAT INJUSTICE!
WON'T BE THE FIRST OF THE WEEK.
NOOOOOOO!

I DON'T LIKE THIS EXECUTION METHOD.
ME, NEITHER. YOU HAVE TO CARRY THE STONE, AND THEN YOU HAVE TO WALK HOME. PFFFT... IN THIS HEAT!
THE WHOLE THING'S UNNECESSARILY ELABORATE.
HH... HH... HH...
YOU!
SHH! SWIM.

DON'T BOTHER WITH THANKS.

THANKS?!
THANKS FOR WHAT? YOU KNOCKED ME OUT! AND BECAUSE OF YOU, I GOT THROWN IN THE RIVER!
BUT I SAVED YOU.

IT WAS THE LEAST YOU COULD DO!
AND NOW I WONDER IF I DID THE RIGHT THING!
YOU DENOUNCED ME TO THE GUARDS!

IT WAS TO SAVE TARID'S HONOR!

CERTAINLY. SURE. WE'RE EVEN, THEN. FAREWELL.
HUH?! WHERE ARE YOU GOING?

I'M LEAVING TOWN. BECAUSE OF YOU, I CAN NO LONGER STAY IN CÓRDOBA.
I'LL TRY TO JOIN TARID.

B... BUT THEN...
IT'S REALLY TARID WHO
STOLE THE BOOKS?!!
OF COURSE!

BUT WHY?!?

TO SAVE THEM.
BY NOW, HE MUST HAVE
REACHED THE TOP OF THE HILLS,
IF YOUR MULE IS ALL RIGHT.
MY...
MY MULE?!

TARID HAS
MY MULE??
PFFF.
OF COURSE.
WASN'T THAT
OBVIOUS?

BUT
THEN... HE
DOESN'T STAND
A CHANCE!
WHY NOT?

THAT'S THE WORST
MULE IN THE HISTORY
OF HUMANITY!

I WOULD HAVE
WARNED YOU IF
YOU'D GIVEN ME
ENOUGH TIME!

A MULE IS A MULE. GOODBYE.
I'M COMING, TOO!

HUH?! OUT OF THE QUESTION.

NOW LEAVE ME ALONE.

WHERE DO YOU WANT ME TO GO?! BECAUSE OF YOU, I'M SENTENCED TO DEATH IN CÓRDOBA AND I HAVE NOTHING!

YOU'LL BE LESS NOTICEABLE WITH ME.

A WOMAN SHOULDN'T GO AROUND ALONE.
I KNOW ALL ABOUT THAT, THANK YOU.

LET'S GO!
COME ON!

WHO RAISED SUCH A USELESS ANIMAL?!?

HAN! HAN...

WHA...?! WHOA!

CAREFUL!

WATCH YOURSELF, AND...

COME ON, LET'S GO!

I...
I CAN'T...
I NEED... TO...
I CAN'T TAKE IT ANYMORE.
MY FEET HURT.
MY LEGS HURT.
I'M THIRSTY.
AND THIS HILL NEVER STOPS RISING!
WHAT POSSESSED ME TO THINK I WAS CAPABLE OF SUCH A JOURNEY?
ME, WHO HAS NOT LEFT CÓRDOBA IN FORTY YEARS.
I'M A LIBRARIAN, NOT A SMUGGLER.

HUFF...
GNRF...
AAAAAH!!
THAT'S THE TREATISE OF AL-KHWARIZMI, YOU DEMON!
HE'S THE WORLD'S GREATEST MATHEMATICIAN!
GNNNNNNNN!
THIS BOOK CROSSED THE SEA AND WAS BARELY SAVED AFTER A SHIPWRECK!
IT'S NOT GOING TO END UP IN THE STOMACH OF A--
I HATE YOU, YOU STUPID ANIMAL.
AAAHHAH!
CHOMP CHOMP...

THIS GOES DOWN.
THAT GOES DOWN.
ALL OF THIS, TOO. IT GOES.
WE'LL KEEP THIS.
THIS, TOO, JUST IN CASE.
THESE GO DOWN.
ALL OF THIS GOES DOWN.

ARE YOU CRYING?

WHY ARE YOU CRYING?

DON'T YOU SEE WHAT'S HAPPENING? THE BOOKS...

YEAH. YOU STOLE THE BOOKS, AND NOW...

THEY'LL BURN THEM ALL!!

THE WORLD'S LARGEST, GREATEST LIBRARY! UP IN FLAMES!
WHAT?!!

WHO WOULD DO SOMETHING LIKE THAT?!
YOUR CHILDHOOD FRIEND!

AMIR?! BUT...
HEY! WAIT FOR ME! WAIT!

Madinat al-Zahra,
palace of Caliph Hisham.
Cordoba, 8km
AH, AMIR! MY DEAR VIZIER!
MY RESPECTS, O COMMANDER OF THE BELIEVERS.
LEAVE US ALONE, MOTHER.
AMIR, I'M TOLD THERE'S SOMETHING GOING ON AT THE LIBRARY.
I'M TOLD BOOKS ARE GOING TO BE DESTROYED.

IT'S ONLY A LIGHT REFRESHMENT OF THE PLACE, O LORD.
WE NEED SPACE FOR NEW WORKS.
WE'RE GETTING RID OF A FEW OLD, WORTHLESS GRIMOIRES.
REALLY?
YOU KNOW HOW MUCH MY FATHER AND GRANDFATHER LOVED THAT LIBRARY, DON'T YOU? THEY DEDICATED THEIR LIVES TO IT. AND A LOT OF MONEY, TOO, I THINK.
I KNOW THIS ALL VERY WELL, BECAUSE I'VE OFTEN CONTRIBUTED TO ITS DEVELOPMENT ALONGSIDE THEM.
MAYBE I SHOULD GO AND SEE WHAT'S GOING ON OVER THERE?
THAT SEEMS RECKLESS TO ME, REVERED CALIPH.
AS WE SPEAK, THE FATIMIDS ARE CONSPIRING TO HARM YOU.
JUST THIS WEEK, TWO ASSASSINS WERE CAPTURED AT THE PALACE GATES.
THE FATIMIDS? AGAIN?

YES, AGAIN, O CALIPH. YOU ARE MUCH SAFER BEHIND THE WALLS OF MADINAT AL-ZAHRA. I'LL HAVE YOUR GUARD REINFORCED.
AS FOR THE LIBRARY, DON'T WORRY. I'LL LOOK AFTER IT.
A "REFRESHMENT," YOU SAID?
MY FATHER AND GRANDFATHER ENLARGED IT, BUT NEVER "REFRESHED." WOULD THEY HAVE APPROVED THIS REFRESHMENT?

I BELIEVE SO, COMMANDER.
ABD AL-RAHMAN III AND AL-HAKAM II, PEACE BE UPON THEM, WERE, FIRST AND FOREMOST, SERVANTS OF GOD.

AND THESE ARE PIOUS WORKS THAT WE'RE WELCOMING TO THE SHELVES. MANY OF THE BOOKS PREVIOUSLY ACCUMULATED NO LONGER HAVE THEIR PLACE.
DON'T LET ALL THIS TROUBLE YOU.

WHAT DO YOU THINK OF THE NEW SLAVES I SENT TO YOU?

THEY'RE SUBLIME! AND EXCELLENT MUSICIANS.
AND THAT NEW WINE FROM THE LOWER ALPS?
A DELICIOUS TRAP.
HEEHEE.
I'M TOLD YOU'RE VERY FOND OF IT, IN FACT...

I'D LIKE TO HEAR YOUR THOUGHTS ABOUT DECORATION OF THE WOMEN'S QUARTERS. DON'T YOU THINK IT'S HIGH TIME TO RETHINK IT?
I SUPPOSE YOU AREN'T WRONG...

IS THERE ANY NEWS ON MY... OTHER BUSINESS?
OTHER BUSINESS?
THE MESSENGER I EXPECT FROM SEVILLE.

STILL NOTHING, GRAND VIZIER.
HE SHOULD HAVE ARRIVED YESTERDAY. WHAT AN UNFORTUNATE SETBACK.
I HOPE NOTHING'S HAPPENED TO HIM.

WHAT EXACTLY DOES THIS MYSTERIOUS MESSENGER BRING YOU?
AURORA.

HE BRINGS WHAT I NEED TO MAKE PEOPLE FORGET THA I'M NOT THE CALIPH.

WHAT I NEED TO REIGN SUPREME.
OH? WITHOUT SHARING?

YOU KNOW EXACTLY WHAT I MEAN.

STILL SNOOZING, THIS ONE.
LAZY!
GOOD
FOR
NOTHING!
WAKE UP!
ON YOUR FEET!

AAAAAAAH!

OOOUUUGH...
WHAT IN THE WORLD...?

I DOZED OFF!

THE MULE!
WHERE IS SHE?!

SOMEONE MUST HAVE STOLEN HER!

WHAT A GOOD-FOR-NOTHING I AM!

IT'S IMPOSSIBLE
AND IT'S POSSIBLE
DARNITOHCRUD IT'S NOT POSSIBLE OH
POSSIBLE IT'S NOT
IT'S NOT POSSIBLE IT'S NOT POS
IMPOSSIBLE OHHNONONONO
NONONONO

UP HERE, MAYBE...

HAAAAN!

Hi HAAAAN!
MY MULE!

Hi HAA^^

Hi HAAAN!

Hi HAAAAN!!

HAAAAN!
HiHAAAAANN!

HEY!

GET AWAY, YOU ROTTEN DOGS FROM THE PITS OF HELL!

I'M GOING TO TEACH YOU...
MPF!

YAAAAAH!

BACK!

WOOOOOOOOP!

GET BACK!
BACK!

WHAT...?
ARRRRF!

HYAAAAAAH!
LUBNA?!?
YAAAAH!
CLEAR OUT!
PSSHHHT!
KAI!

YOU SHOULD HAVE STAYED UNDER TREE-COVER. IT'S LUCKY THAT I'M THE ONLY ONE WHO KNOWS WHICH DIRECTION YOU WENT.
KAÏ!
KAÏ!
HOW DID WE CATCH UP TO YOU SO QUICKLY WHEN YOU LEFT SEVERAL HOURS BEFORE US?
IT'S THAT STUPID MULE!

FIRST IT REFUSES TO MOVE, THEN IT DISAPPEARS!
SHE'S THE DEVIL. I'VE ALWAYS SAID IT. YOU'LL HAVE TO KILL HER.

WHO IS THIS?

YOU DON'T RECOGNIZE ME?

WELL, I...
NNNOOOOO?
MARWAN?
NNOOOOO?!
YES!
YES!
YOU DIRTY, MISERABLE LITTLE THIEF!
I'LL CUT OFF YOUR HANDS! TRAITOR!
HEY!

APPARENTLY, HE HASN'T FORGOTTEN YOU...
HOW COULD I?! HE'S THE WORST DISCIPLE I EVER HAD!
LAZY!
NO DISCIPLINE!
LIAR! ROGUE!

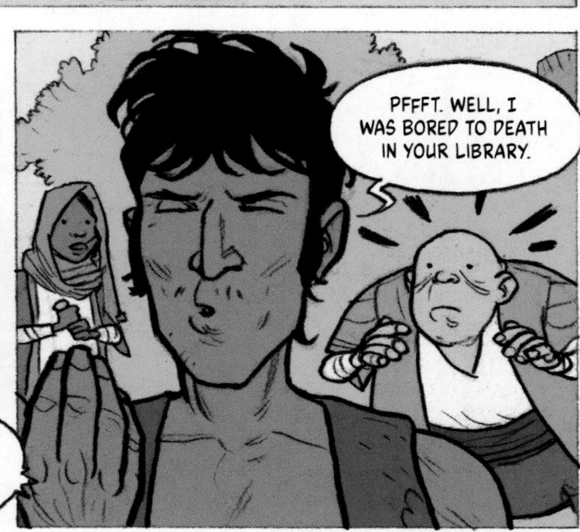
PFFFT. WELL, I WAS BORED TO DEATH IN YOUR LIBRARY.

YOU WERE BORED...?! THE GREATEST SCIENTIFIC
ENTER IN THE WEST! THE TEMPLE OF ALL KNOWLEDGE, ATTRACTING SCHOLARS AND PHILOSOPHERS FROM BAGHDAD AND CONSTANTINOPLE!
IDIOT! ILLITERATE!

WHAT ARE YOU DOING HERE WITH SUCH A PERSON?! I THOUGHT I TOLD YOU TO STAY IN CÓRDOBA!
IT'S TOO DANGEROUS!

I WAS UNDER SUSPICION. IT WAS BETTER I LEAVE.

DO YOU EVEN KNOW WHAT HE DID TO ME?!

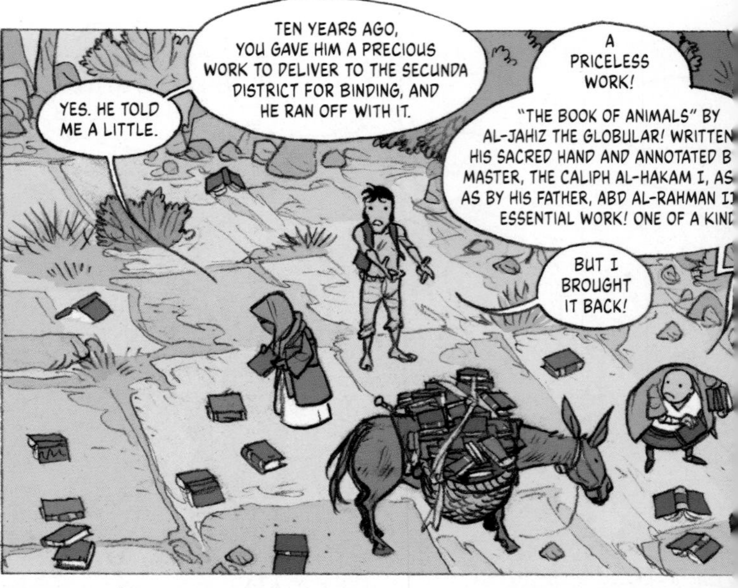
YES. HE TOLD ME A LITTLE.
TEN YEARS AGO, YOU GAVE HIM A PRECIOUS WORK TO DELIVER TO THE SECUNDA DISTRICT FOR BINDING, AND HE RAN OFF WITH IT.
A PRICELESS WORK!
"THE BOOK OF ANIMALS" BY AL-JAHIZ THE GLOBULAR! WRITTEN HIS SACRED HAND AND ANNOTATED B MASTER, THE CALIPH AL-HAKAM I, AS AS BY HIS FATHER, ABD AL-RAHMAN I ESSENTIAL WORK! ONE OF A KIND
BUT I BROUGHT IT BACK!

WHAT?
I WAS GOING TO RETURN IT TO YOU LAST NIGHT, BUT THIS WOMAN KNOCKED ME OUT.

WITH A VOLUME OF "THE BOOK OF SONGS."
BUT... BUT WHY NOW, FOR GOD'S SAKE?

WELL, TO GET YOUR FORGIVENESS! I CAME BACK TO CÓRDOBA TO BEGIN A NEW LIFE, AND I WANTED TO START BY MAKING AMENDS FOR MY MISTAKES.
WAS THAT YOU LAST NIGHT IN THE GARDENS?

YES! I THOUGHT I'D ENTER THROUGH THE WINDOW, LIKE I DID WHEN I SNUCK OUT AS A KID.
YOU... YOU WERE SNEAKING OUT?!

WELL, OF COURSE! JUST LIKE ALL THE OTHER SLIGHTLY RESOURCEFUL APPRENTICES AT THE LIBRARY!
HUH! BUT... REALLY?
WHAT KIND OF WORLD DO YOU LIVE IN, TARID?

SO, WHERE IS THIS BOOK?

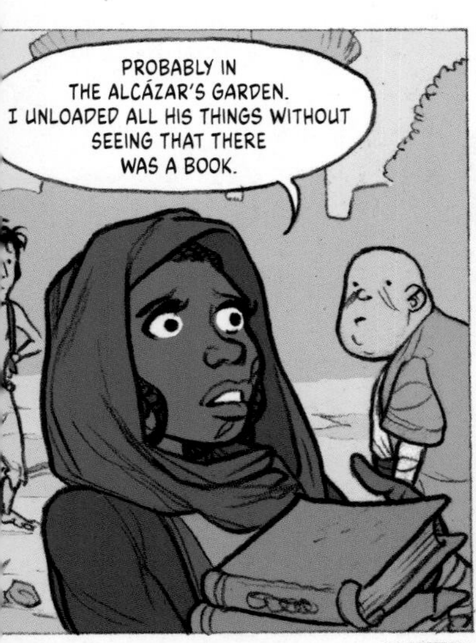
PROBABLY IN THE ALCÁZAR'S GARDEN. I UNLOADED ALL HIS THINGS WITHOUT SEEING THAT THERE WAS A BOOK.

WELL DONE! MAGNIFICENT! IT'LL END UP ON THE PYRE, LIKE ALL THE OTHERS! WHAT AN IDIOT!

HEY! LET GO, YOU!
I THOUGHT I WAS DOING THE RIGHT THING!
GET OUT OF HERE! I NEVER WANT TO SEE YOU AGAIN!
HNNNNN!

RIP

-KHWARIZMI AGAIN?! DOES SHE HAVE AGAINST MATHEMATICS?

STUPID MULE!

FINE, I'LL LEAVE. AS SOON AS YOU GIVE ME BACK MY MULE.
EXCUSE ME?

I CAME TO CÓRDOBA BECAUSE THE NEW VIZIER IS MY FRIEND.
I WANTED TO USE THIS FRIENDSHIP TO BECOME SOMEONE IMPORTANT, WHO WOULD NEVER AGAIN NEED TO STEAL TO LIVE. AS A RESULT, I WAS THROWN INTO THE GUADALQUIVIR!

MY PLAN IS RUINED. I CAN NO LONGER GO TO CÓRDOBA. I'VE GOT NOTHING LEFT. EXCEPT THIS MULE.
SHE MAY BE STUPID, BUT SHE'S MY ONLY ASSET.

SO GIVE HER BACK. THIEF.

ARE YOU SURE THIS IS YOUR MULE?

WHAT'S THAT?
I THINK YOU STOLE THIS MULE.
H... HOW DARE YOU?! I WOULDN'T DO THAT!
CAN YOU SWEAR TO ALMIGHTY GOD THAT YOU DIDN'T STEAL IT?
I... GULP... YEAH, I... THAT IS...
HAHAHAHA! YOU'RE A PITIFUL THIEF! UNABLE TO LIE PROPERLY!
I'M ACTUALL VERY GOOD AT LY I LIE ALL THE TI BUT... NOT IN FR OF GOD...
PFFFF... ALL LIES ARE LIES BEFORE GOD. FIGURE IT OUT.
A LITTLE THIEF! THAT'S WHAT YOU WERE, AND THAT'S WHAT YOU ARE.
YOU STARTED BY STEALING "THE BOOK OF ANIMALS," AND NOW YOU'RE STEALING THE WORST MULE IN THE WORLD.
TOMORROW, YOU'LL BE STEALING GOAT DROPPINGS.
THE DAY AFTER TOMORROW, YOUR HEAD WILL BE ON A PIKE. YOU COULD HAVE BECOME A GOOD COPYIST, BUT THIS IS THE LIFE YOU'VE CHOSEN.
THAT'S IT. NOW GO AWAY.
HOW DID YOU KNOW ABOUT THE MULE?
THE SWORD IS WORTH MORE THAN THE MULE. IF IT WAS REALLY YOURS, YOU'D KNOW THAT.
YOU WOULD HAVE CLAIMED THE SWORD INSTEAD.

PERFECT. I'LL BE OFF, THEN.
POF

AND DON'T WORRY. I WON'T TURN YOU IN.
I CAME TO MAKE AMENDS. I WANTED YOU TO HAVE A BETTER MEMORY OF ME.
YOU FAILED. DISAPPEAR!

GO TO HELL, YOU BITTER OLD EUNUCH.

CHOKE ON YOUR DAMN BOOKS!

HERE'S WHAT I THINK OF YOUR BOOKS!
HUH...?!?

IT'S NOT GOING TO HOLD UP.
YOU'RE RIGHT. WE NEED MORE ROPES.
THERE ARE TOO MANY BOOKS.
THERE ARE **NOT** TOO MANY BOOKS.

I HAVE IT!
WHAT DOES THIS RAKE WANT NOW?

I HAVE IT!

"THE BOOK OF ANIMALS"!
WHAT?!

AH, IT'S... THIS IS IT!
IT'S A MIRACLE!

I MUST'VE PUT IT BACK ON THE MULE WITH THE OTHER BOOKS WITHOUT REALIZING. INCREDIBLE...

SO, WHAT
O YOU SAY TO
HAT? I SAVED
T, AFTER ALL.
BE QUIET. DON'T TALK. LET ME SAVOR THIS MOMENT.
YOU CAN'T IMAGINE WHAT THIS BOOK REPRESENTS.
A LITTLE BOY RECEIVED A SOLID BEATING OVER THIS BOOK...
HE'S GONE MAD, HASN'T HE?
I DON'T THINK SO.

IT WON'T HOLD UP. YOU NEED MORE ROPE.
I KNOW

AND BLANKETS.
I KNOW! IT'S TOO HEAVY.

THE ROPES ARE HURTING THE MULE. THAT'S WHY SHE'S NOT MOVING.

NOTHING DOING.
TOC TOC
SHE'S NOT MOVING BECAUSE SHE'S ROTTEN! TRUST ME.
I TRAVELED WITH HER FOR SEVERAL DAYS, AND SHE'S ROTTEN.

SHE'S LAZY, UNDISCIPLINED, WILY...

BIRDS OF A FEATHER FLOCK TOGETHER.
VERY FUNNY.

THANK YOU FOR RETURNING IT.
CAN I HAVE MY MULE BACK NOW?

NO.
WE NEED HELP.
YOU HAVE TRAVELING EXPERIENCE, AND WE DON'T. SO IF YOU COME WITH US, I PROMISE YOU COMPENSATION ON ARRIVAL.
WHERE ARE YOU GOING?

TO BATALYAWS.*

BATALYAWS?!?
WITH A LOAD LIKE THIS, IT WILL TAKE AT LEAST TWO WEEKS!
YOU'RE WEARING SLIPPERS!
YOU KNOW WHAT IT'S LIKE ON THE ROAD! THERE ARE BEASTS, BANDITS, PROBABLY SOLDIERS LOOKING FOR YOU...

DO YOU AT LEAST HAVE FOOD?
NO.

AND NO MONEY TO BUY IT. A THIEF WOULD BE WELCOME.

ADAJOZ

WHAT DO
YOU THINK?

THERE'S STILL WORK TO BE DONE, BUT FOR A FORMER SCRIBE, IT'S ENCOURAGING.
THIS SWORD IS THAT OF ABD AL-RAHMAN III, ISN'T IT?

AND THAT OF AL-HAKAM II, WHO NEVER USED IT. HISHAM ENTRUSTED IT TO ME AS A TOKEN OF HIS TRUST.
IT'S A GOOD BLADE, ISN'T IT?
I BELIEVE SO, YES. A LITTLE HEAVY, PERHAPS, BUT VERY BEAUTIFUL.

TEACH ME EVERYTHING YOU KNOW, MASTER-AT-ARMS. IT'S URGENT.
YOUR COURIER FROM SEVILLE HAS FINALLY ARRIVED, GRAND VIZIER.

I HOPE HE HAS A GOOD EXCUSE FOR THIS INCOMPETENCE.

HE HAS A BROKEN ARM AND LEG, O GRAND VIZIER. A PASSING CARAVAN FOUND HIM ON THE SIDE OF THE ROAD.
AH...

FORGIVE ME, GRAND VIZIER, FOR NOT PROSTRATING PROPERLY BEFORE YOU.
I FORGIVE YOU, YAKUB. SPEAK PLAINLY, FOR TIME IS SHORT.
WHAT I SENT YOU FOR... DO YOU HAVE IT?

I HAD IT, GRAND VIZIER, BUT...
...SADLY, I DON'T HAVE IT ANYMORE.
CLING
RAAAAH!!!
YOU'RE GOING TO TELL ME EVERYTHING, AND DON'T LEAVE OUT ANY DETAILS. I WANT TO KNOW EVERYTHING.
EVERYTHING.
MARWAN! MARWAAAAN!
WHERE IS HE, THAT KLUTZ?
10 years ago...

DID YOU MAKE THIS COPY?

WE CAN NO LONGER HEAR OURSELVES TURNING THE PAGES...
MY RESPECTS, O MIGHTY CALIPH.
FORGIVE ME FOR DISTURBING YOUR PEACE.
I'VE BEEN ENTRUSTED WITH THIS YOUNG MAN'S TRAINING, AND I'M DESPERATE TO MAKE HIM A DECENT COPYIST.
LET'S SEE...
YES, IT'S... HOW SHOULD I SAY IT? PERFECTIBLE.
IT'S JUST THAT IT'S GREEK...
WHAT'S YOUR NAME, BOY?
MARWAN, VENERABLE CALIPH.
ARE YOU A SLAVE?
NO, BUT HE'S A CHILD OF THE STREETS. IT WAS MUHAMMAD AMIR, YOUR ADMINISTRATOR, WHO CONVINCED ME TO GIVE HIM A CHANCE HERE.
HE SAYS THE BOY HAS A FINE AND LIVELY MIND.
BUT HE SPENDS HIS TIME RUNNING AROUND AND AVOIDING HIS DUTIES.

HA HA HA!
MY FATHER, ABD AL-RAHMAN, ONLY WANTED FEMALE COPYISTS. HE SAID MEN WEREN'T METICULOUS ENOUGH FOR THE JOB. PERHAPS HE WAS RIGHT.

YOUR FATHER WAS RIGHT IN EVERYTHING, MAJESTY.
DO YOU REALIZE, LITTLE ONE, THE CHANC YOU'VE BEEN GIVEN?

THERE IS ONLY ONE LIBRARY GREATER THAN THIS IN THE ENTIRE WORLD, AND THAT IS IN BAGHDAD, VERY FAR FROM HERE.
LOOK AROUND. YOU ARE SURROUNDED BY SENSITIVE, WELL-EDUCATED PEOPLE. AND IF YOU WORK HARD, AT THE END OF YOUR TRAINING, YOU WILL ALSO BE ABLE TO TAKE PART IN THIS GREAT WORK. WHAT DO YOU SAY?

I WILL DO AS YOU WISH, VENERABLE CALIPH. MY ONLY DESIRE IS TO SERVE YOU.

IT IS GOD WE SERVE IN THIS BUILDING, NOT ME.

WE GIVE THANKS TO GOD WHEN WE TRANSLATE THE WORLD'S SCIENTISTS AND POETS INTO ARABIC...
...PERSIAN, HEBREW, SYRIAC, HINDI, LATIN, OR GREEK!
AND WE MAKE COPIES OF THEIR WORKS SO THAT AS MANY PEOPLE AS POSSIBLE CAN DISCOVER THEM.
IT'S GOD WE SERVE WHEN WE TAKE THE MEASURE OF THE COMPLEXITY OF HIS WORK AND PASS IT ON TO OUR FELLOW MAN.
IT'S GOD WE SERVE WHEN WE MAKE ISLAM THE MOST ADVANCED, EDUCATED, AND OPEN CIVILIZATION IN THE WORLD.

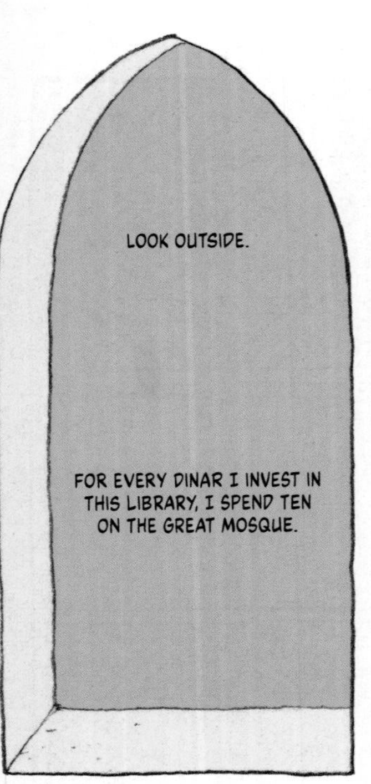

LOOK OUTSIDE.
FOR EVERY DINAR I INVEST IN THIS LIBRARY, I SPEND TEN ON THE GREAT MOSQUE.

CÓRDOBA IS THE LARGEST CITY IN THE WESTERN WORLD. AS SUCH, IT MUST HAVE THE LARGEST MOSQUE.
GOD IS GREAT...
NOTHING IS TOO GRAND FOR HIM.

AND WE'RE ALSO BUILDING PUBLIC UNIVERSITIES, BECAUSE MUSLIMS NEED TO BE EDUCATED. MY FATHER BUILT FIFTEEN OF THEM.

IF GOD WILLS IT, I WILL DO MORE.

IN THIS LIBRARY, YOU AND I AND TARID ARE ALL THE SAME...

...HUMBLE SERVANTS.

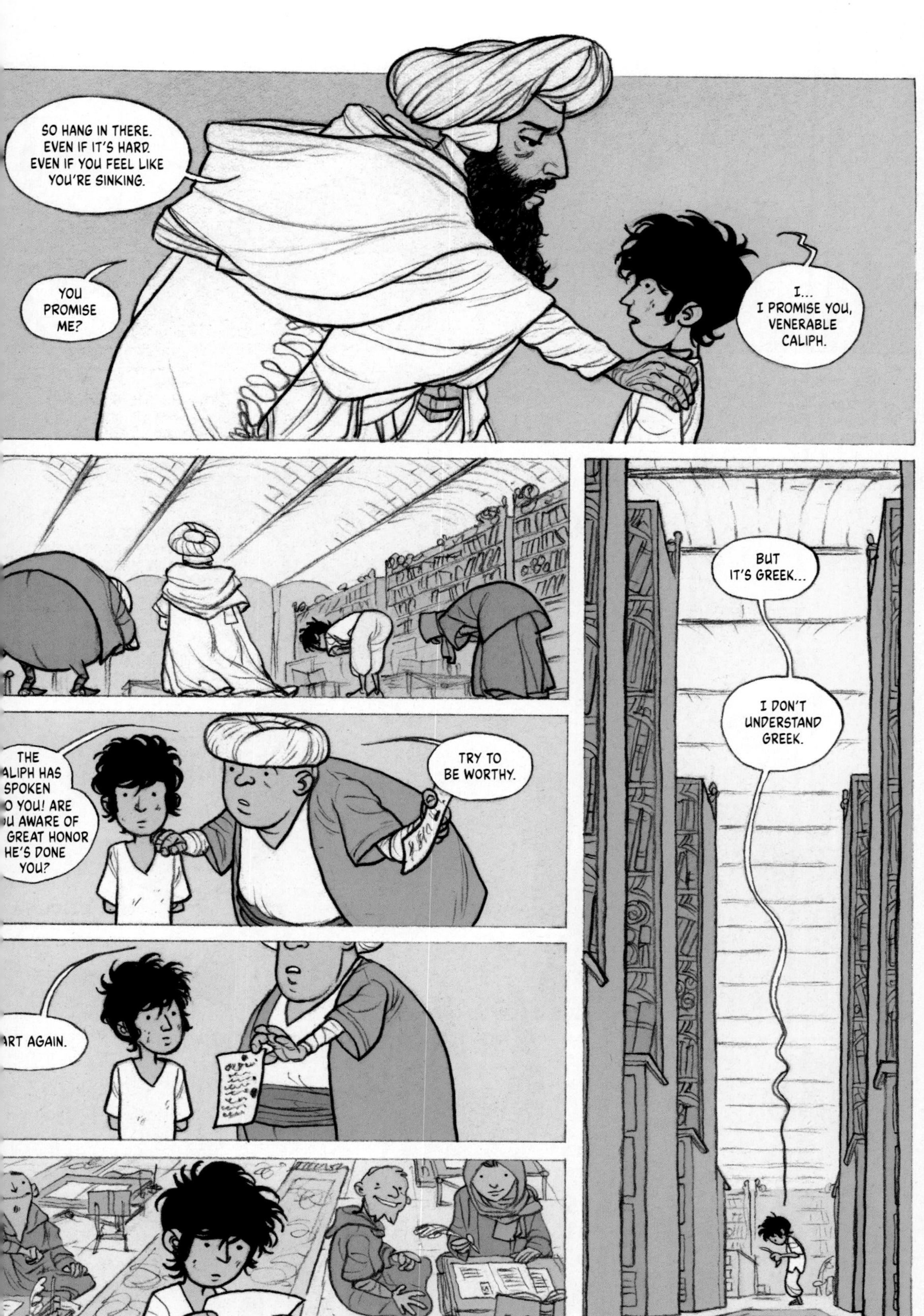
SO HANG IN THERE. EVEN IF IT'S HARD. EVEN IF YOU FEEL LIKE YOU'RE SINKING.
YOU PROMISE ME?
I... I PROMISE YOU, VENERABLE CALIPH.
THE ALIPH HAS SPOKEN O YOU! ARE U AWARE OF GREAT HONOR HE'S DONE YOU?
TRY TO BE WORTHY.
ART AGAIN.
BUT IT'S GREEK...
I DON'T UNDERSTAND GREEK.

WHY BATALYAWS?
THE KING OF BATALYAWS HAS A PASSION FOR SCIENCE AND POETRY. HE NEVER CAME TO CÓRDOBA WITHOUT PAYING A VISIT TO OUR LIBRARY, WHICH HE HELD IN GREAT ESTEEM. HE'LL RECEIVE THESE BOOKS WITH RESPECT AND HONOR, AND THEY'LL BE SAFE IN HIS OWN LIBRARY.
COMPLETE DELUSIONA
DO YOU HAVE A BETTER IDEA? WHERE WOULD YOU HAVE US GO?
León
Castile
Navarre
Caliphate of Córdoba
Batalyaws
Córdoba
Algeciras
Ifriqiya
I DON'T KNOW... SOUTH, ACROSS THE STRAIT.
IN IFRIQIYA? WHERE REIGN THE FATIMIDS, SAVAGES WHO MOCK THE SCIENCES?! AND THE BERBERS, THOSE IGNORANT BRUTES?!
AND ANYWAY, I WON'T BE ABLE TO BOARD AT ALGECIRAS. IT'S VIZIER AMIR'S HOMETOWN. HE COMPLETELY CONTROLS IT, AND--
AND...?
AND I'VE BEEN ON A BOAT BEFORE. IT MADE ME HORRIBLY SICK!
MMMH... AND BY THE... NEITHER...
LET'S SEE, LET'S SEE...
?
WHAT...? WHAT ARE YOU STILL DOING, LUBNA?
I CAN'T HOLD IT!

NO!
STOP THAT MULE!

SHE'S SLIPPED!

BROUF

NOTHING...OOF... WILL BE SPARED...AOUCH... FOR ME. NOTHING.

SHE REALLY WANTS UP THIS STEEP SLOPE.
ONCE SHE'S UP, SHE'LL HAVE TO...
WELL, HELP ME HOLD THE BOOKS AND LET HER UP.

...STOP.

SHE WANTED A DRINK! THIS MULE'S STRONG!

THE BOOKS! WE HAVE TO COLLECT THEM!
WOUHOUUUUUH! YEEEEEEEEESSSSS!

SPLASH
THEY'RE THE SAME, THOSE TWO.
HEHEH... HE'S FUNNY.

FUNNY? WHAT'S FUNNY ABOUT HIM? HE'S A DONKEY!
GLUP
GLUP

AAAAAH! THE MULE! SHE'S... RIGHT IN THE MIDDLE...

...OF THE WATER...

ONE WRONG MOVE, AND THE BOOKS ARE RUINED!
TAKE THIS!

WHAT ARE YOU DOING?

HELLO, DEAR...

...COME THIS WAY, SWEET MULE...
...COME, COME. LOOK AT THESE APPETIZING THISTLES. COME ON...

ZIIP

SPLASH

GOT IT!
IT SEEMS I HAVE A KNACK FOR SAVING BOOKS.

I DON'T KNOW WHERE YOU'RE GOING, TARID...
...BUT IF YOU THINK A FAT BOOKWORM CAN CROSS AL-ANDALUS AND ESCAPE MY ARMIES...
...YOU'RE DELUDING YOURSELF.

"The rat... looks for... small birds and other small creatures, as well as... eggs and bread..."
BROOD, NOT BREAD. CAN'T YOU READ?
I HAVEN'T READ ANYTHING IN YEARS, SORRY TO REPORT...
"... and brood. But at the same time it must... hunt, it must avoid its... its Pr... predators, such as snakes and birds of prey..."
EVERYBODY KNOWS THIS! IS THIS ALL THAT'S IN YOUR PRECIOUS "BOOK OF ANIMALS"?

THAT AND MANY OTHER THINGS. AL-JAHIZ THE GLOBULAR COMPILED ALL OF ARISTOTLE'S OBSERVATIONS ON THE ANIMAL WORLD AND ENRICHED THEM WITH HIS OWN COMMENTS. IT'S A COLOSSAL WORK.
WHY'S HE CALLED "THE GLOBULAR"?
BECAUSE HIS EYES WERE BUGGING OUT OF HIS HEAD.
HA! HA!

IT GIVES US INFORMATION ON FOOD CHAINS AND THE SURVIVAL TECHNIQUES OF VARIOUS SPECIES.

BUT ABOVE ALL, IT DEFINES THAT SCIENTIFIC RIGOR MUST BE BASED ON DOUBT.

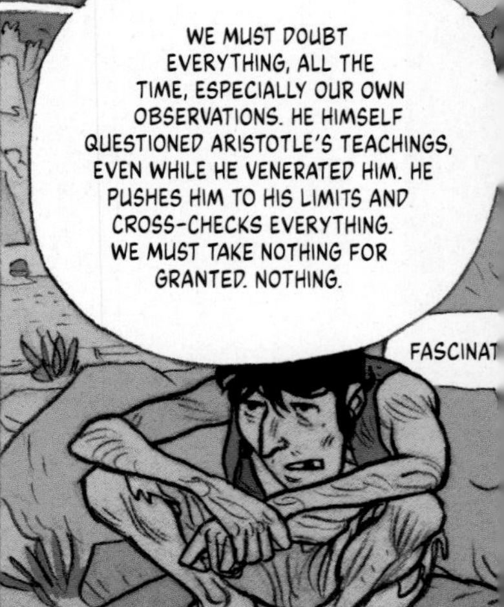
WE MUST DOUBT EVERYTHING, ALL THE TIME, ESPECIALLY OUR OWN OBSERVATIONS. HE HIMSELF QUESTIONED ARISTOTLE'S TEACHINGS, EVEN WHILE HE VENERATED HIM. HE PUSHES HIM TO HIS LIMITS AND CROSS-CHECKS EVERYTHING. WE MUST TAKE NOTHING FOR GRANTED. NOTHING.
FASCINAT

FOR EXAMPLE, HE REFUTES THE EXISTENCE OF DRAGONS AND CHIMERAS. HE REFUTES THE COMMONLY HELD BEDOUIN BELIEF THAT SPOTTED HYENAS CHANGE SEX EVERY YEAR.
"Our actions for our descendants must equal that of our ancestors in our favor. Our knowledge is more extensive than that of previous generations, but must be less than that of our posterity."
YOU SEE? WE HAVE TO PASS ON OUR KNOWLEDGE TO...
RR Z Z Z Z
HE FELL ASLEEP.
YOU SHOULD DO THE SAME.
I'M NOT SLEEPY. WHICH BOOK DID WE LOSE IN THE CREEK?

SEEMS LIKE IT WAS THE TREATISE ON THE TRANSLATED WORKS OF GALEN, BY HUNAYN IBN ISHAQ.
SIGH... A TRAGEDY. SUBLIME CALLIGRAPHY. BEAUTIFUL TEXT.
I WANTED TO SAVE IT FROM THE FIRE, BUT IT PERISHED IN THE WATER.

A NUMBER OF BOOKS SUFFERED FROM DROPS, AS WELL. BINDINGS ARE BROKEN, AS ARE SPINES. AT THIS RATE, WE'LL REACH BATALYAWS EMPTY-HANDED.

THIS MULE! IF WE REACH OUR DESTINATION, I'LL KILL IT WITH MY OWN HANDS.

ANYWAY, WHAT'S SO SPECIAL ABOUT THIS COPY OF "THE BOOK OF ANIMALS"?

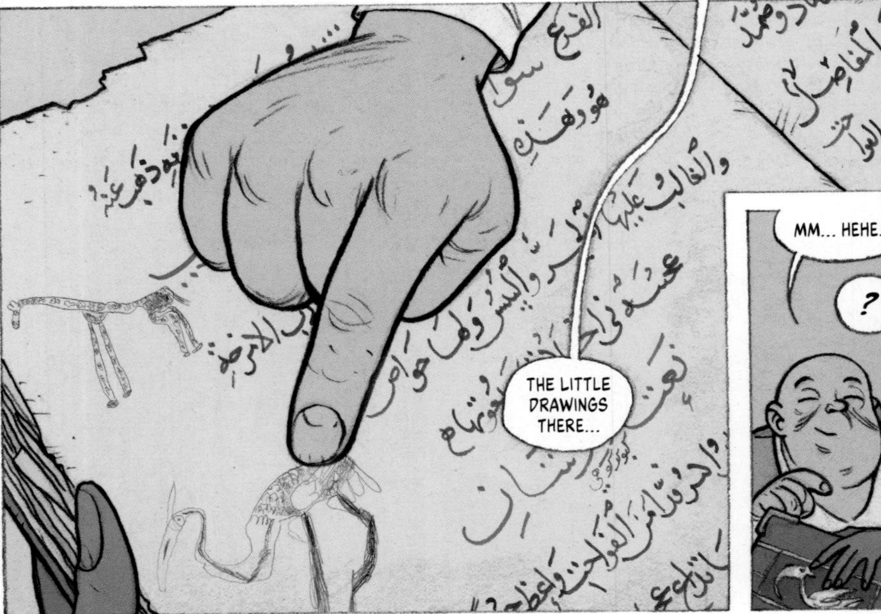
THE LITTLE DRAWINGS THERE...
MM... HEHE.
?

AAAAAAH!
AAAAAII!! I'M SORRY!
40 YEARS AGO...
AAH!
SCREAM ALL YOU WANT! I'LL TEACH YOU TO RESPECT THE BOOKS!
HERE!
EASY, MY SON!
EDUCATED EUNUCHS ARE EXPENSIVE. WHAT HAS HE DONE?
HE DEGRADED AL-JAHIZ'S "THE BOOK OF ANIMALS"!
DEGRADED, HM? LET'S SEE.
WHAT'S YOUR NAME, CHILD?
TARID, O GREAT CALIPH.
SNIFF

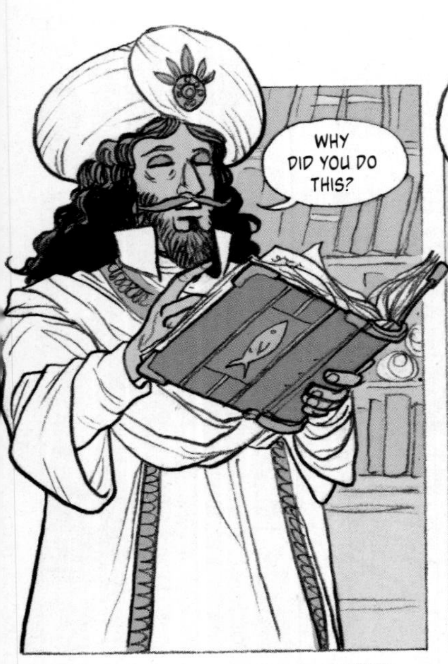
WHY DID YOU DO THIS?

IT'S BECAUSE, WHEN I READ THE TEXT, I IMAGINE ALL THE ANIMALS IT DESCRIBES...
AND I'VE NEVER SEEN MOST OF THEM...
SO, I COMPARED IT WITH THE PASSAGES FROM ARISTOTLE THAT HE MENTIONS, BUT IT'S NOT ALWAYS MADE CLEAR, SO...
SO...
SO, I MAKE UP THE REST.

SCOUNDREL.
YOU... READ GREEK?

SNIFF. AND LATIN, GREAT CALIPH.
AND WOULD YOU SAY YOU LIKE THIS BOOK?

I LOVE IT, GREAT CALIPH!
IT'S MY FAVORITE BOOK, AND I'M WORK ON A COMPLETE COP

THAT DOESN'T GRANT YOU PERMISSION TO DAMAGE THE ORIGINAL, YOU LITTLE FOOL!
I THINK HE GETS IT.

OH, *YES!* I UNDERSTAND, GREAT CALIPH.

I'D LIKE YOU TO DO ME A FAVOR, YOUNG TARID.
IN THE FUTURE, TAKE CARE OF THIS BOOK LIKE THE SKIN OF YOUR OWN BUTT. ALL RIGHT?
YES, GREAT CALIPH. I WILL CHERISH IT ALL MY LIFE, GREAT CALIPH.
CAN YOU LIEVE IT? LATIN, EK, AND ARABIC AT HIS AGE...
AND HE'S NOT A BAD ARTIST, EITHER. HAHA.
YOU THINK I SHOULDN'T HAVE BEATEN HIM?
HE'LL REMAIN DOCILE.
YOU'VE DONE VERY WELL. YOU MADE ME HIS SAVIOR.

GNAP

NO. IT'S NOT POSSIBLE...
HE CAN'T... NO... NO...

MUHAMMAD AMIR, YOU DOG!
MAY YOU BE DAMNED FOR WHAT YOU'VE DONE, YOU HEAR ME?!

MAY YOU BE DAMNED FOR WHAT YOU'VE DONE!!!

?

?
DAMNED!

YOU AND YOUR DESCENDANTS...
...AMIR THE TRAITOR.

YOU'RE JUST A...

...A...

TARID!

THE TIME FOR SCIENTIFIC CHATTER IS OVER!
THESE SACRILEGES ONLY DISTANCE THE BELIEVER FROM THE MESSAGE OF GOD!
GONE ARE THE DAYS WHEN WE WERE BLINDED BY THE HERITAGE OF ANCIENT, LOST CIVILIZATIONS!
GONE ARE THE DAYS OF THE GREEKS, THE JEWS, THE CHRISTIANS!
ENOUGH OF ALL THAT!
HERE, PEOPLE OF CÓRDOBA, IS THE ONLY BOOK WORTH READING!
THE ONE YOU MUST WORSHIP! THE ONE THAT CONTAINS ALL ANSWERS TO ALL QUESTIONS!
GOD IS GREAT!
GOD IS GREAT!

O GRAND VIZIER, DO YOUR DUTY!
GIVE THANKS TO GOD BY RIDDING THE WORLD OF THESE BLASPHEMOUS WRITINGS! SET THE FINAL PYRE ALIGHT!
MAY IT BE DONE ACCORDING TO GOD'S WILL!
WE WILL VISIT EVERY HOUSE IN CÓRDOBA!
WE WILL DESTROY ALL BOOKS THAT GO AGAINST THE TRUTH REVEALED TO THE PROPHET MUHAMMAD!
ALL THAT IS NECESSARY TO RECORD IN WRITING, THE PROPHET HAS REVEALED TO US!
THE REST IS JUST CONFUSION!
GOD IS GREAT!

GOD is GREAT!
GOD is GREAT!
IT IS NOT BY DIPPING ONE'S QUILL IN INK THAT ONE SERVES GOD.

IT IS BY DIPPING HIS BLADE IN THE BLOOD OF INFIDELS!

HE'S BREATHING PEACEFULLY. IN MY OPINION, HE'S JUST TIRED.
IN MY OPINION, IT'S MORE SERIOUS THAN THAT.
I DON'T KNOW IF HE CAN SURVIVE WHAT'S GOING ON OUT THERE.

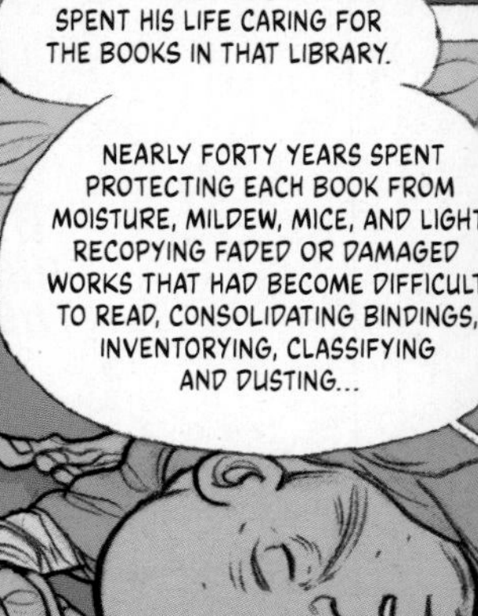
TARID HAS SPENT HIS LIFE CARING FOR THE BOOKS IN THAT LIBRARY.
NEARLY FORTY YEARS SPENT PROTECTING EACH BOOK FROM MOISTURE, MILDEW, MICE, AND LIGHT, RECOPYING FADED OR DAMAGED WORKS THAT HAD BECOME DIFFICULT TO READ, CONSOLIDATING BINDINGS, INVENTORYING, CLASSIFYING AND DUSTING...

HE KNOWS NOTHING ELSE. IT'S HIS HEART THAT BURNS OVER THERE.
HE'S THE ONE THEY'RE BURNING.

I THINK YOU'VE GOT THE WRONG IDEA. THIS SMOKE... IT COULD BE SOMETHING ELSE ENTIRELY.
WE DON'T KNOW WHAT IT IS.

WE KNOW EXACTLY WHAT IT IS. IT'S AN ABOMINATION.
IT'S THE END OF A DREAM.

IT MAKES NO SENSE! WHY WOULD AMIR DO THIS? THE WHOLE WORLD VALUES SUCH A LIBRARY!
YOU WANT A REASON?

THE REASON FOR ATROCITIES IS ALWAYS THE SAME: POWER.
OKAY, BUT...
I DON'T FEEL LIKE TALKING, MARWAN.

FORGIVE ME. TONIGHT, I JUST WANT TO MOURN EVERY BOOK THAT'S GONE UP IN SMOKE.
HOW... HOW MANY DO YOU THINK THERE ARE?

DON'T YOU REMEMBER ANYTHING?
I WAS SMALL! IT NEVER INTERESTED ME!

ASK TARID WHEN HE WAKES UP. BUT I'D SAY...

... SEVERAL HUNDRED THOUSAND.

EACH UNIQUE.
EACH MAGNIFICENT.
EACH ANNOTATED WITH COMMENTARY BY THE GREATEST MINDS OF OUR TIME...

SEE THERE? HE'S ALREADY DEAD.
HE'S SOFT. I ALWAYS SAID SO.
WE HAVEN'T TOUGHENED HIM UP ENOUGH.
COME ON.
REMEMBER THAT, WHEN WE FOUND HIM, HE WAS HALF-DEAD FROM THE COLD.
AND HE SURVIVED.
WHEN THE MERCHANTS BEAT HIM TOO, HE SURVIVED.
HE WAS VERY SWOLLEN, HOWEVER.
BLOATED.
WE BEAT HIM A GOOD DEAL OURSELVES, AS WELL.

OH, YEAH!
EVERY DAY. HE HAD TO GET EVERYTHING INTO HIS HEAD.
WELL, IT FINALLY FIT. IT WASN'T EASY.
THIS IS A DIFFERENT KIND OF INJURY, THOUGH.
HE SHOULD TOUGHEN UP! HE'S SOFT!
HE'S SLEEPING.

AH! YOU'RE UP? FEELING BETTER?

WE'LL... WE'LL BE LEAVING SOON, I GUESS. WE SHOULD... WHERE'S LUBNA?

I'M HERE.

SORRY, TARID.
I LOOKED EVERYWHERE
FOR YOUR SLIPPER, BUT
I COULDN'T FIND IT.

NEVER MIND.
LET'S JUST GO.

WE'RE...
LEAVING ALREADY?
AREN'T WE HAVING
LUNCH?
WE DON'T
HAVE ANYTHING
FOR LUNCH.

I CAN CATCH FISH
BY HAND, YOU KNOW!
WE COULD...

PFFFF...

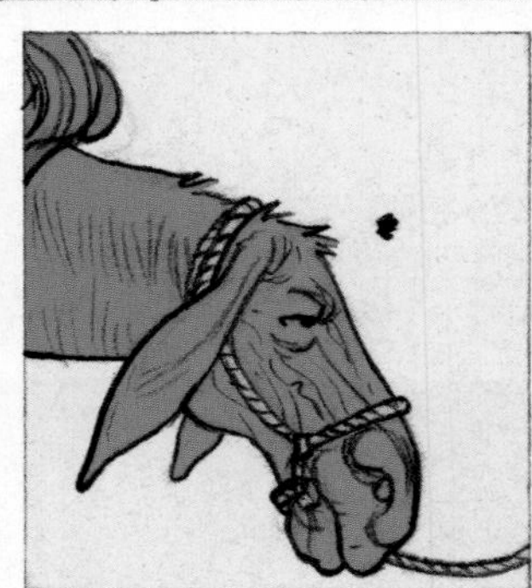

ARE WE GOING TO WALK THE WHOLE WAY LIKE THIS, WITHOUT SAYING A WORD?
MMMH.

IT'S SINISTER. YOU SEE, THIS IS EXACTLY WHY I LEFT THE LIBRARY. I COULDN'T STAND THE SILENCE...

DID YOU LIKE THE ATMOSPHERE? THIS GLOOM? SERIOUSLY?

YES, I LIKED IT! UNLIKE YOU, I WAS BORN A SLAVE. A WOMAN AND A SLAVE! AND DESPITE THAT, I WAS LUCKY ENOUGH TO RECEIVE AN EDUCATION, BECAUSE AN EDUCATED SLAVE HAS GREATER VALUE.
I WAS TAUGHT TO READ, TO WRITE, SYRIAC, PERSIAN, MUSIC, AND CALLIGRAPHY... ALL TO MAKE A HANDSOME PROFIT WHEN I WAS SOLD.
AND I WAS SOLD!
I FOUND MYSELF IN THE SERVICE OF CALIPH AL-HAKAM II. CAN YOU BELIEVE IT?
I LIVED HAPPILY IN THE COPYIST WOMEN'S HOUSING, AND TO THIS DAY, INSTEAD OF GUTTING FISH OR SPENDING MY DAYS BEATING LAUNDRY IN THE RIVER WITH A DOZEN BRATS CLINGING TO MY DRESS...
...I WAS LUCKY ENOUGH TO ENJOY THE BLESSED SILENCE OF THE LIBRARY...
...TO INDULGE IN THE SILENT ART OF CALLIGRAPHY...
...AND TO READ HISTORY'S GREATEST THINKERS.
BROOOOM
COME AND HELP ME.
IT WON'T STAY UPRIGHT. IT'S NEVER GOING TO LAST.

WHAT WE'RE DOING IS FUTILE. FUTILE AND RIDICULOUS.
COME ON. WE'LL PUT THEM BACK.

WHAT'S THE POINT?! THEY'LL FALL AGAIN AND AGAIN!

ACCORDING TO RAZI'S TREATISE ON ANATOMY THAT YOU HOLD, WE HAVE IN EACH FOOT 26 BONES, 16 JOINTS, AND 107 LIGAMENTS...
...AND THEY ALL HURT EXCRUCIATINGL BAD!
NOT TO MENTION THE SPLINTERS.

OH, YOU'VE SAVED A RAZI!

I CAN LEND YOU MY SLIPPERS, IF YOU WANT...?

IT'S NOT ABOUT MY SLIPPERS, LUBNA!
I CAN'T DO THIS. I'VE NEVER WALKED SO MUCH! EVERY MUSCLE IN MY BODY HURTS.
I HAVE NO STRENGTH LEFT! I'M FAT AND SOFT! I'M WEAK!
I'M... I'M HUNGRY.

I'M HORRIBLY HUNGRY.

OF COURSE! WE LEFT WITHOUT LUNCH.
SNIFRL...

OH, NO! HORSEMEN!

WE HAVE TO
GET EVERYTHING
PICKED UP!

QUICKLY!

FORGET IT!
WE DON'T HAVE TIME!

WHAT THE
HELL'S WRONG
WITH YOU?!

TURN
THE MULE!
WHAT?

TRUST ME!
TURN THE MULE.

PEACE BE UPON YOU,
VALIANT SOLDIERS.
WHOAWHOA...
OUUUUCHIE!

PEACE BE UPON YOU, PEASANT.
IS THIS YOUR WIFE?

YES, SHE'S VERY SICK. FEVER! AND STRANGE BOILS BETWEEN HER LEGS.

BOILS? UGHHHH...

I DON'T KNOW WHAT'S WRONG WITH HER, SO I'M TAKING HER TO CÓRDOBA TO SEE A DOCTOR.
WE'RE LOOKING FOR A RUNAWAY SLAVE.

A PLUMP EUNUCH IN HIS FIFTIES, TRAVELING WITH A MULE.
HAVE YOU COME ACROSS HIM?

N... NO...
ANYWAY, HE WON'T GET FAR.

PIGEONS WERE DISPATCHED TO ALL GUARD POSTS AND CITIES.
FROM BATALYAWS TO TULAYTULAH*, HE'LL FIND NO REFUGE. THERE'S A PRICE ON HIS HEAD EVERYWHERE.

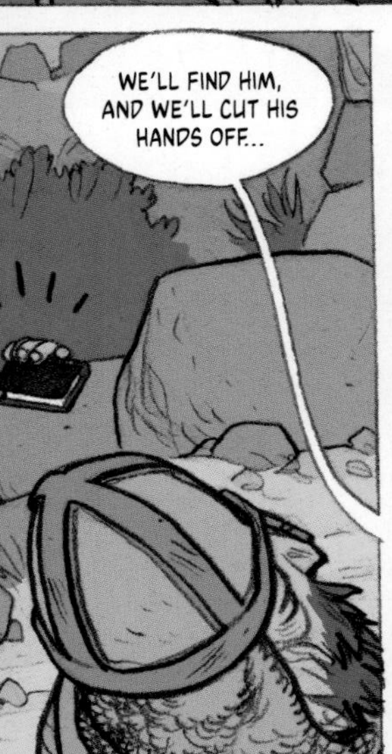
WE'LL FIND HIM, AND WE'LL CUT HIS HANDS OFF...

...BEFORE LEAVING HIM TO DIE IN THE SUN.

Hi HAAAN!

*TOLEDO

HAHA!
HAHAHA!

CONTROL YOUR MULE, PEASANT!
S... SORRY... SAY, WHAT EXACTLY DID THIS EUNUCH DO?

HE'S A THIEF. HE'S MADE THE VIZIER VERY ANGR
COME ON, THEN. OFF WE GO!

"STRANGE BOILS BETWEEN HER LEGS"?! HOW MORTIFYING!

YOU DON'T KNOW SOLDIERS. BELIEVE ME, I HELPED YOU AVOID A MUCH GREATER SHAME.
WHA...?
OH...

AND NOW YOU'VE SEEN HOW WELL I LIE IF I'M NOT ASKED TO SWEAR BEFORE GOD!

THEY'RE GONE, TARID. WE CAN GET MOVING AGAIN.

MOVING? TO GO WHERE? YOU HEARD THEM! EVERYBODY'S LOOKING FOR ME TO CHOP ME UP!

EVERYTHING'S RUINED!
HE HAS A POINT. THE LORD OF BATALYAWS WILL TURN US IN TO PLEASE THE VIZIER.
THEY'RE GOING TO CRUSH US LIKE FLIES.

BZZZ

BZZZZ

BZZP
RAAAAH! THIS FLY, RUBBING IT IN MY FACE!

BZZ

BZZZ
PSSHHTT! GO AWAY!
BUT...?!
I SHOULDN'T HAVE SAID "FLY."

STOP, YOU WRETCH!
WHAT? IS THIS YOUR FLY OR SOMETHING?
OF COURSE IT'S MY FLY.
BZT.
IT'S OUR FLY!
IT'S THE MOST IMPORTANT FLY IN THE WORLD.
HELLO, PRETTY LITTLE FLY.
YOU... YOU'RE SCARING ME, TARID...
WHAT HAVE YOU LEARNED FROM ME, DONKEY?!
AIIIEUH!
ONE WONDERS! COME ON!
HEEEEEYY!

THAT FLY IS THE FLY OF ALL WRITERS, THINKERS, SCIENTISTS, AND ARTISTS!
IT'S THANKS TO THIS LITTLE, BLACK FLY THAT WE CLIMBED OUT OF THE DARK!
LET GO OF ME, DAMMIT! LUBNA, CAN'T YOU SEE HE'S GONE CRAZY?
AH! LOOK! SEE THAT?
?!?
UH...SOME SORT OF BALL...
SOME SORT OF BALL...
"KEKIDION" IN GREEK! HIPPOCRATES WAS ALREADY TALKING ABOUT IT NEARLY A THOUSAND YEARS AGO! IT'S LIKE A PIMPLE GROWING ON THE SKIN OF AN OAK TREE, AN ALLERGY.
IT'S AN OAK GALL, YOU IDIOT!
THE FLY HAS LAID ITS EGGS AT THE BASE OF THE BUD, AND THE TREE IS TRYING TO DEFEND ITSELF AGAINST THE PRESENCE OF THE EGGS. AND VOILÀ! A GALL!
THE GALL GROWS AND PROTECTS THE FLY'S LARVA. WHEN THE FLY HAS COMPLETED ITS TRANSFORMATION, IT MAKES A HOLE IN THE SHELL AND LEAVES THE GALL.
SO WHAT?

IT'S BY GRINDING THESE GALLS THAT THE BEST INK IS MADE.

IT'S COOKED WITH GUM ARABIC AND IRON SULFATE!

NO INK IS AS STABLE OR LASTS AS LONG AS INK MADE FROM OAK GALLS.
SNIFF
SNIFF

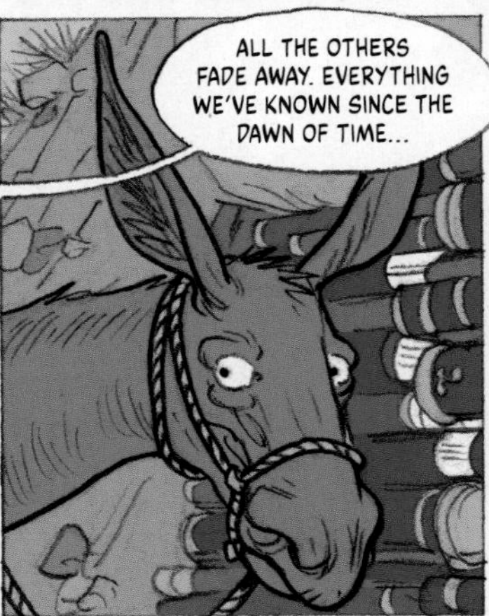
ALL THE OTHERS FADE AWAY. EVERYTHING WE'VE KNOWN SINCE THE DAWN OF TIME...

...WE KNOW BECAUSE WE'VE MANAGED TO WRITE IT DOWN WITH AN INK THAT STANDS THE TEST OF TIME.

AND IT'S ALL THANKS TO THIS FLY! MAY IT BE BLESSED FOR ETERNITY!
AND IT LANDED ON YOUR STUPID NOSE.
SO WHAT?

SO, IT'S A SIGN! DON'T YOU SEE?

THERE ARE HUNDREDS, NO, THOUSANDS OF SPECIES OF FLIES!
AND IT'S PRECISELY THIS ONE THAT COMES TO REST ON YOUR NOSE JUST WHEN WE'RE ON THE VERGE OF GIVING UP!

LUBNA, DO YOU AGREE WITH THIS DELUSIONAL INTERPRETATION?
COMPLETELY. IT'S A SIGN. WE CAN'T GIVE UP NOW.
THE SCIENTISTS AND ARTISTS OF CENTURIES PAST ARE WATCHING. COME ON, WE'VE GOT TO RELOAD THE MULE.
BUT WE DON'T EVEN KNOW WHERE WE'RE GOING!
THAT'S TRUE. BUT THE ADVANTAGE IS THAT WE CAN'T GET LOST.
RAAAAH!
THIS ROTTEN MULE TAKES ADVANTAGE OF THE SLIGHTEST OPPORTUNITY TO...
GNNNN!
WHAT...?
STILL AL-KHWARIZMI!!! BUT... WHY?! WHY THIS BOOK?
WHAT'S AN AL-KHWARIZMI?
HE WAS A GREAT SCIENTIST. HE LIVED IN BAGHDAD, AND HE UNDERSTOOD EVERYTHING ABOUT THE WORLD.
AND THIS MULE ABSOLUTELY WANTS TO EAT HIS CONCLUSIONS. SHE MUST BE IN LEAGUE WITH AMIR!

YOU SEE, THIS IS ANOTHER REASON I RAN AWAY.

WE SPENT ALL OUR TIME CARRYING STACKS OF BOOKS. I COULDN'T TAKE IT ANYMORE.
YOU DON'T HAVE TO TELL ME.

IN THE BEGINNING, I TOO HAD GRAND IDEAS ABOUT COPYIST WORK. I SAID TO MYSELF, "AH, THE WORDS, THE SPIRIT, THE IDEAS..."

BUT I QUICKLY REALIZED THAT IT WAS ALSO LEATHER, PARCHMENT, PAPER, WEIGHT...

ALL THE LIBRARIANS AND BOOK MERCHANTS LOSE THEIR BACKS TO IT.

LIKE THIS POOR MULE.
AND YOU PUT UP WITH IT?

WELL, THAT'S...
IF IT WEREN'T FOR THE WEIGHT OF THE BOOKS, THE READER'S SPIRIT WOULD FLY AWAY!

LAST STACK.

WE'RE OFF.

OUCH. WE'RE RUINED.
WE'LL NEVER GET THROUGH. THERE ARE GUARDS EVERYWHERE.
FORTUNATELY, WE HAVE THIS.
YOU, UH... YOU WANT TO ATTACK THIS FORT WITH ONE SWORD BETWEEN THE THREE OF US?
BETTER THAN THAT.
TSZING!

UGHHHH...
IT'S HORRIBLE TO BE A WATCHMAN IN PEACETIME. HORRIBLE.
WE SCAN AND SCAN, BUT WE KNOW FULL WELL THAT NOTHING IS GOING TO HAPPEN.
I CRAVE CHANGE.
STOP COMPLAINING. AT LEAST WE HAVE SOMETHING TO LOOK FOR NOW, THAT ARCHIVIST AND HIS MULE...
YEAH, SURE... HE'S NOT GOING TO PASS HERE, RIGHT UNDER OUR NOSES. ANYWAY, THE ONLY PEOPLE AROUND HERE ARE OLD WOMEN GOING TO THE FIELDS.
LOOK, HERE COME SOME MORE...

WHAT DO YOU THINK THEY WANT WITH THIS ARCHIVIST?
TO CUT HIS HANDS OFF, PROBABLY. HE STOLE BOOKS, THEY SAY...
STEALING BOOKS... WHAT A NUT!
YOU SAID IT. IS THERE ANY MORE HERB CHEESE?
I THINK SO. DOWNSTAIRS.
KEEP LOOKING, I'LL GET IT.
I'M LOOKING, I'M LOOKING.
UGHH...

SO, TELL ME...
HAS LIFE OUTSIDE OUR
LIBRARY'S "SINISTER" WALLS
FULFILLED YOUR DESIRES?
FROM
A CERTAIN
PERSPECTIVE,
YES.

I'M MADE FOR THE
GREAT OUTDOORS.
IN RECENT YEARS,
I'VE LIVED HUMBLY,
ENJOYING SIMPLE
PLEASURES: A NAP IN THE
GRASS, A BATH IN THE
RIVER, A GRILLED FISH...

BUT HOW DID YOU
AFFORD CLOTHES? HOT
MEALS? YOU CAN'T LIVE ON
GRILLED FISH ALONE...
WELL...

I MIGHT'VE... PILFERED...
LEFT AND RIGHT...
HERE AND THERE...
I SEE.

BUT NOT OFTEN!
AND NEVER MORE
THAN NECESSARY.

BUT IN THE END, I GREW TIRED OF THIS LIFE...
ONE DAY, I DECIDED ENOUGH WAS ENOUGH.
THAT'S WHEN YOU DECIDED TO RETURN TO CÓRDOBA.
NO.
THAT'S WHEN I DECIDED TO STEAL SOMETHING RARE AND GET RICH IN ONE FELL SWOOP.

SO ONE NIGHT, IN SEVILLE, I BROKE INTO THE PROPERTY OF A WEALTHY MERCHANT WHO'D JUST RETURNED FROM THE ORIENT.

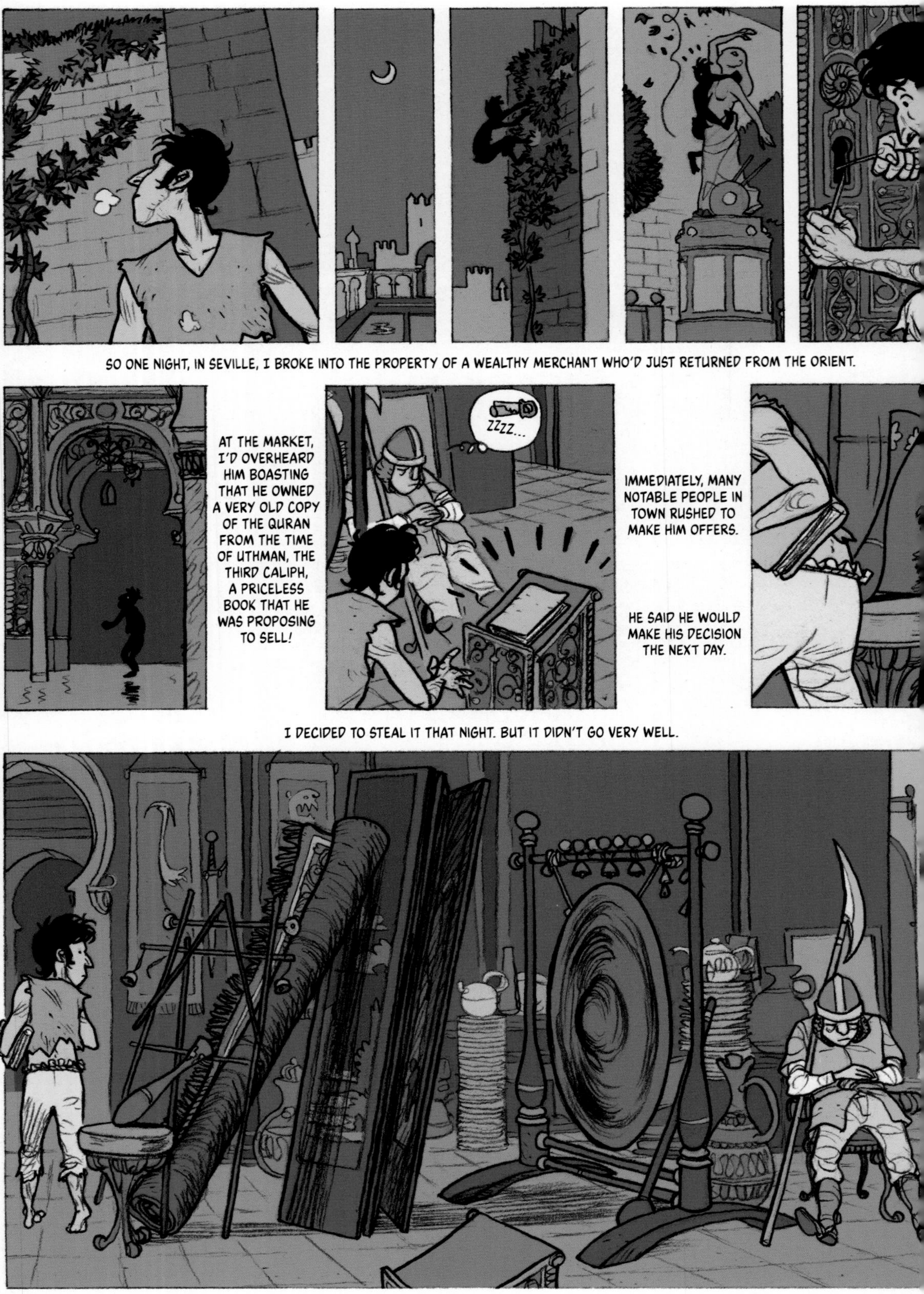

AT THE MARKET, I'D OVERHEARD HIM BOASTING THAT HE OWNED A VERY OLD COPY OF THE QURAN FROM THE TIME OF UTHMAN, THE THIRD CALIPH, A PRICELESS BOOK THAT HE WAS PROPOSING TO SELL!

IMMEDIATELY, MANY NOTABLE PEOPLE IN TOWN RUSHED TO MAKE HIM OFFERS.

HE SAID HE WOULD MAKE HIS DECISION THE NEXT DAY.

I DECIDED TO STEAL IT THAT NIGHT. BUT IT DIDN'T GO VERY WELL.

HAVE MERCY! MERCY! I'LL NEVER DO IT AGAIN!

I WOULD LIKE TO SEE THE OBJECT OF THE CRIME.

BEHOLD, YOUR HONOR. A PRICELESS COPY OF THE QURAN WRITTEN IN MEDINA, JUST SIXTEEN YEARS AFTER THE PROPHET'S DEATH.

THE WRITING IS NOT THE SAME AS THAT USED BY THE EARLY CALIPHS.
THE SCRIPT USED AT THAT TIME WAS HIJAZI, AND THIS QURAN IS WRITTEN IN KUFIC.
IT'S A BEAUTIFUL QURAN, BUT YOU CAN BE SURE IT'S NO MORE THAN A HUNDRED YEARS OLD.
IT'S NOT TRUE! HE'S LYING!
HOW DO YOU KNOW ALL THIS?

WHAT?!
HE TRIED TO STEAL
FROM ME!
I COULD SAY THE
SAME. YOU TRIED TO
STEAL FROM US!
WE'LL
GIVE YOU THE
BENEFIT OF THE
DOUBT.
YEAH, RIGHT.
ME?! BUT I'M
A VICTIM, TOO! I
DIDN'T KNOW!

COME ON,
TAKE YOUR BOOK
BACK...

WE WON'T
CUT OFF YOUR
HANDS TODAY,
YOUNG MAN.
WHA...?
REALLY? THANK
YOU! THANK
YOU!

DON'T
MENTION
IT.

LOCK HIM IN
THE DUNGEON
FOR A FEW
YEARS...
HUH?!

WHO WAS THE MAN WHO RECOGNIZED YOU?
THE ONE TO WHOM I SOLD "THE BOOK OF ANIMALS" BY AL-JAHIZ THE GLOBULAR TEN YEARS AGO!
HE HAD JUST SET UP IN SEVILLE.
YOU OWE HIM A DEBT OF GRATITUDE.
THOSE MANGY DOGS LEFT ME LANGUISHING IN THE DUNGEON FOR THREE YEARS.
GOSH. I IMAGINE THAT GAVE YOU TIME TO THINK.
YOU DON'T THINK IN A DUNGEON. YOU SUFFER.
MY THOUGHTS SOLIDIFIED ON THE NIGHT AFTER MY TRIAL.
I SAID TO MYSELF: IF YOU STILL HAVE HANDS, IT'S THANKS TO TARID. THANKS TO WHAT HE TAUGHT YOU...
...AND THANKS TO THE RESPECTABILITY THAT SURROUNDS HIS NAME.
THAT SURROUND*ED* HIS NAME.
I TOLD MYSELF IT WAS TIME TO CHANGE MY LIFE. IT WAS TIME TO BE HONEST AND DIGNIFIED AGAIN.
ABOVE ALL, I REALIZED THAT I REALLY OWED TARID A LOT.
AND THE BEST THING I COULD DO TO REPAY HIM WOULD BE TO RETURN THE BOOK I STOLE.
"THE BOOK OF ANIMALS"?
EXACTLY. I MADE A VOW TO MYSELF TO TAKE IT BACK AS SOON AS I WAS FREE, AND THAT'S WHAT I DID.
BUT HOW DID YOU GET IT BACK?

WELL, I STOLE IT!

I HAD NO CHOICE! THAT KIND OF BOOK IS WORTH A FORTUNE! AND THE OWNER WASN'T WILLING TO SELL IT, OF COURSE.
BUT I MADE AN OATH TO MYSELF THAT, AFTER THAT, I'D NEVER STEAL AGAIN.

THIS TIME, I WAS SUCCESSFUL, AND I RAN AWAY FROM SEVILLE AND... STRAIGHT TO CÓRDOBA.

Hi HAAAN!!!
RAAAH! JUST KEEP MOVING, YOU DAMN FOOL!

AND THAT WAS YOUR LAST BIT OF THEFT?
YES, THE VERY LAST! I SWEAR!
AND THE MULE?

AH, WELL... THE MULE DOESN'T COUNT. I... I FOUND HER, SO TO SPEAK...
SO TO SPEAK?

YEP! SHE WAS STANDING ON THE SIDE OF THE ROAD, COMPLETELY ALONE.
TSSS.

I SWEAR IT! I SWEAR! BEFORE GOD.

PLIC

HUH?

IT NEVER RAINS IN THIS COUNTRY, SO WHY DID IT HAVE TO RAIN TODAY?!
IT'S JUST A STORM!

THERE!

THIS MUST BE A CARAVAN SHELTER. THERE ARE REMNANTS OF THE FIRE.

PFFF... LOOK AT THIS...

ALAS, WE CAN'T EAT BOOKS.

KR
YES, BUT...

WHAT ARE YOU DOING?! STOP IT!
YOU UNDERSTAND THAT WE'RE TRYING TO SAVE THESE BOOKS FROM BURNING, DON'T YOU?!
HEY!
JUST A FEW PAGES! IT'S ALL BANGED UP ANYWAY.
I MUST AT LEAST KNOW WHAT IT IS FIRST... ***EH?!*** "THE BOOK OF PENETRATING EXPLANATION," BY IBN MASARRA! THE FIRST PHILOSOPHER OF CÓRDOBA!
HE WAS SO FAR AHEAD OF HIS TIME THAT HE FINISHED HIS LIFE HIDDEN AT THE BOTTOM OF A CAVE. HE, TOO, WAS HUNTED LIKE A DOG.
AND YOU WANTED TO BURN HIS WORK?!
YEAH, AND WHAT ABOUT IT?!
IF WE STAY WET, THE COLD WILL BE UNBEARABLE. WE HAVE TO DRY OURSELVES AND DRY THE BOOKS.
FINE. BUT JUST A FEW PAGES TO START THE FIRE.

WHAT IF WE LEFT THE BOOKS HERE?
THAT'S NO GOOD, IS IT?

WHY NOT? IT'S A BIT LIKE YOUR LIBRARY, THIS CAVE. IT'S DARK, NOT TOO HUMID... WE CAN COME BACK FOR THEM WHEN THINGS CALM DOWN.
AND RODENTS? WHAT ABOUT FUNGI? FLOODS? HAVE YOU THOUGHT ABOUT ALL THAT?
AND WHAT IF THEY NEVER CALM DOWN, THESE "THINGS"?

AND IF YOU'D STUDIED A BIT OF GREEK AND READ PLATO, YOU'D UNDERSTAND THE FOLLY OF TRYING TO HIDE KNOWLEDGE AT THE BOTTOM OF A CAVE!
HUH?
NEVER MIND.

WHERE ARE WE GOING, THEN? HERE'S A MAP OF THE CALIPHATE. I REALLY DON'T SEE WHERE...
سرقسطة
ليون
قرطبة
بطليوس
لشبونة
إشبيلية

HERE. WE GO TO LEON.

HAHAHA!
THIS KEEPS GETTING BETTER!

IT WOULD TAKE MORE THAN A MONTH TO GET TO LEON ON FOOT!
TARID, IT'S A CHRISTIAN KINGDOM!

DIRTY, IGNORANT BARBARIANS WHO EAT PORK!
THEIR LORDS ARE ILLITERATE AND SPEND ALL OF THEIR TIME KILLING EACH OTHER FOR POWER!
THEY LIVE IN GLOOMY, BLACK STONE CASTLES AND SLEEP ON BEDS OF STRAW. THEY'RE ANIMALS!

AND WHY WOULD THEY WELCOME US THERE?
THEY LIVE IN PEACE WITH THE CALIPHATE, AND THEY WON'T RISK DISPLEASING THE VIZIER BY WELCOMING FUGITIVES.
WHAT'S MORE, AS FAR AS WE KNOW, THE NEW KING IS EIGHT YEARS OLD! CAN YOU IMAGINE? OUR LIVES HANGING ON THE DECISION OF A BRAT?

LITTLE RAMIRO WILL WELCOME US, AS HIS FATHER AND I WERE VERY CLOSE FRIENDS.

WHAT?

AD PROELIVM DE SOLIO LEON
SANCHE RE
25 YEARS AGO, WHEN KING RAMIRO II OF LEON DIED, THERE WERE VIOLENT WARS OF SUCCESSION BETWEEN HIS SONS AND THEIR COUSINS.
AFTER VARIOUS BATTLE AND BETRAYALS, SANCH THE YOUNGEST SON, SEIZED THE THRONE.
PANUM REX
GRAVITAS LEX
BUT HE HAD, IT IS SAID, A HEARTACHE THAT HE TRIED TO CURE THROUGH GLUTTONY. HE ATE SO MUCH THAT HE SOON BECAME TOO FAT TO RIDE A HORS
AFTER A CRUSHING MILITARY DEFEAT, LEON'S NOBILITY DECIDED TO DEPOSE HIM.
HIS COUSIN ORDOÑO IV KNOWN AS "THE WICKEI TOOK THE CROWN.

ISOLATED AND TURNED AWAY BY NAVARRE AND CASTILE, SANCHO CAME TO ASK THE FORMER CALIPH ABD AL-RAHMAN III FOR HELP.

ABD AL-RAHMAN AGREED TO HELP SANCHO WEAKEN LEON.

HE ENTRUSTED HASDAI, HIS FAMOUS PERSONAL PHYSICIAN, WITH THE MISSION OF HELPING SANCHO LOSE WEIGHT AND GET BACK IN THE SADDLE.

WHAT'S THAT HAVE TO DO WITH YOU?
AT THE TIME, I WAS VERY YOUNG, BUT HAD ALREADY BECOME AN IMPORTANT SCRIBE IN THE LIBRARY, WORKING DAILY WITH ASDAI AND THE MONK NICOLAS ON A TRANSLATION OF DIOSCORIDES' WORKS THAT THE PATRIARCH OF CONSTANTINOPLE HAD OFFERED TO THE CALIPH.

DIOSCO.. WHATNOW?
...RIDES. DIOSCORIDES. HE WROTE THE MOST IMPORTANT TREATISE ON MEDICINAL PLANTS OF ALL TIME. YOU'D KNOW THAT IF--
DON'T YOU START, TOO!
WHERE WAS I...?

HASDAI REALLY LIKED ME, BUT HE DIDN'T LIKE MY FATNESS, AS IT SOMETIMES MADE MY WORK DIFFICULT. THEN, HE HAD AN IDEA...

HE MADE ME A DIETING COMPANION, SO THAT SANCHO THE FAT WOULDN'T SUFFER ALONE.

OUR LIVES BECAME A LIVING HELL. UNDER HASDAI'S WATCH, SANCHO AND I SUFFERED A THOUSAND TORMENTS. AFTER EXHAUSTING DAYS, WE WOULD SILENTLY SHARE AN INFAMOUS VEGETABLE BREW BEFORE COLLAPSING, EXHAUSTED AND DEPRESSED. THIS TORTURE LASTED FOR WEEKS.

WE SUPPORTED EACH OTHER THROUGH THIS TERRIBLE ORDEAL.

MOVED BY THE SUFFERING I WAS EXPERIENCING, THE WOMEN OF THE COPYIST'S QUARTERS ORGANIZED A SURPRISE MEAL FOR ME.

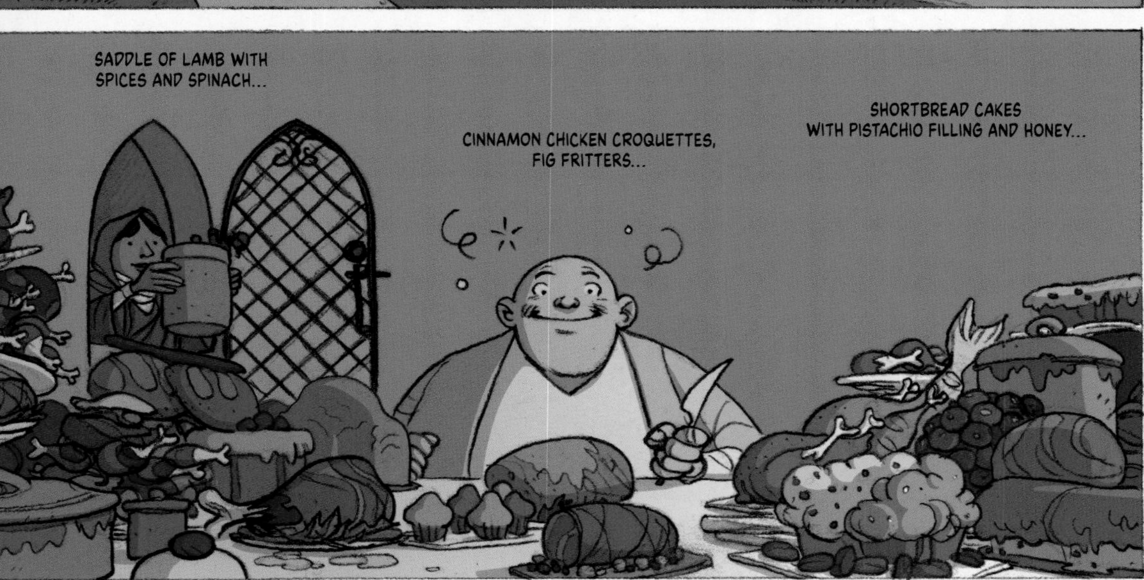
SADDLE OF LAMB WITH SPICES AND SPINACH...
CINNAMON CHICKEN CROQUETTES, FIG FRITTERS...
SHORTBREAD CAKES WITH PISTACHIO FILLING AND HONEY...

I WAS ABOUT TO BEGIN MY FEAST, BUT GUILT CAME UPON ME BY SURPRISE.

I IMAGINED POOR SANCHO TRYING TO SLEEP THROUGH THE NOISE HIS EMPTY STOMACH WAS MAKING.

I FELT SO SORRY FOR HIM THAT I RISKED EVERYTHING TO GO AND GET HIM.

WE ATE IT ALL! AND THEN WE DRANK!

AND THEN WE GOT SICK!

THE NEXT DAY, WE WERE PUNISHED.

BUT WHILE WE WERE EATING THE PASTRIES...

...WE'D COEXISTED IN COMPLETE BLISS.
PFFFFFF... OOOHOOHOHOHOHO HO!

WHAT? THAT EVEN UNITED US FOR LIFE. YOU WOULDN'T UNDERSTAND! WHEN SANCHO LEFT, IT WAS A VERY EMOTIONAL DEPARTURE.
WE HAD BECOME BROTHERS!

AND HE REGAINED HIS THRONE?
YES, WELL... HM. HE WENT BACK ON HIS PROMISES TO ABD AL-RAHMAN. THERE HAVE BEEN WARS SINCE.

ARE YOU SERIOUS?
YOU REALLY WANT TO GO
ALL THE WAY TO LEON?

BECAUSE
OF PISTACHIO
SHORTBREAD?

LEON, YES.
TOMORROW.

GOODNESS,
THAT STORY MADE
ME HUNGRY.

LET'S
HOPE THE SON
OF SANCHO THE
FAT LOVED HIS
DADDY.

YOU'VE PUT
ON A LITTLE WEIGHT
SINCE THEN, HAVEN'T
YOU?
GNAGNAGNA.
GO TO SLEEP.

HE'S GROWING DISCOURAGED, ISN'T HE?
HE STILL SAYS HE'S HUNGRY.
HE WAS VERY OFTEN HUNGRY. AND MUCH MORE THAN THAT. HE DOESN'T REMEMBER. HE WAS SMALL.
HE REMEMBERS IT WELL. IT FRIGHTENS HIM.

ALL THIS, TOO, IS FOR YOUR FRIEND AMIR.

HE'S HAVING A HUGE NEW PALACE BUILT...

...BIGGER THAN MADINAT AL-ZAHRA, THE PALACE OF THE CALIPHS.

AND HE'S LOWERED THE TAXES ON OLIVE OIL, TO POLISH HIS IMAGE WITH MERCHANT GUILDS.

AH. MORE SOLDIERS LOOKING FOR US.

LOTS OF EXPENSES AND LITTLE INCOME. THIS IS HOW AMIR RUNS THE CALIPHATE.
DO YOU KNOW HOW ONE BALANCES SUCH A BUDGET?
NO.
BY WAGING WAR.

WE'VE BEEN AT PEACE WITH THE CHRISTIAN KINGDOMS FOR SEVERAL DECADES.
YES. ABD AL-RAHMAN SIGNED THE PEACE TREATIES. HIS SON REINFORCED THEM, AND THE ARAB LORDS DON'T WANT WAR.
THAT'S WHY AMIR BROUGHT IN HORDES OF BERBER MERCENARIES FROM IFRIQIYA.

THEY'RE LOOKING FOR US IN THAT CARAVAN.

TO BURN THE LAST BOOKS. SO THAT THE WAR CAN BEGIN.
COME ON.

MARWAN?

IMBECILE!
HE'S NOT SERIOUS! HE DOESN'T THINK...

OH, HE...
HEEEEEY!
THERE IT IS.

ACK...!
YES! GO LEFT!
NO, NO!
LEFT!

NOW WHERE'D THAT SIMPLETON GO?
ARF...
GN...
RAAAH...
BAD LUCK.
SAY, YOU'RE A LOUSY THIEF, AREN'T YOU?
YOU THINK IT WORKS OUT EVERY TIME?
THINK IT'S ALL IN FUN, THIEV-ING?
YOU'VE MADE ME HORRIBLY HUNGRY WITH THOSE CHICKENS. I REALLY GOT MY HOPES UP.
SORRY.

HOW DID YOU BECOME FRIENDS, YOU AND AMIR?
OUR FAMILIES WERE NEIGHBORS.
MY FAMILY WAS POORER THAN AMIR'S, BUT OUR FATHERS DECIDED TO MAKE THE PILGRIMAGE TO MECCA TOGETHER. THEY NEVER RETURNED.
THEY'RE SAID TO HAVE DIED NEAR TRIPOLI. PROBABLY ATTACKED BY BRIGANDS. WE BECAME CLOSE THEN. HE NEVER LET ME DOWN.
HE WAS ALWAYS KIND.
KIND? WHEN AL-HAKAM II DIED, AMIR HAD HIS TWO BROTHERS MURDERED...
...AND HE IMPRISONED JA'FAR, HIS FELLOW VIZIER, AND HAD ALL HIS POSSESSIONS CONFISCATED.
AL-HAKAM II
HE CREATED THE POWER VACUUM AROUND YOUNG HISHAM.
I... I DON'T UNDERSTAND.
THIS MAN, THE ONE YOU'RE DESCRIBING...
...IS NOT MY FRIEND.

FLAC

YOU LOOK CONCERNED, AMIR.
IT'S THE EUNUCH WHO MAN-AGED THE LIBRARY...
HE RAN AWAY WITH SOMETHING PRECIOUS.
MY HUSBAND, AL-HAKAM, SPENT ALL HIS TIME IN THAT LIBRARY. TOO MUCH TIME. YOU SHOULD KNOW IT, SINCE YOU'VE REPLACED HIM IN HIS BED.
SOME GREAT WORK?
HIS QUEST FOR KNOWLEDGE HAD NO END. WHAT AMBITION OF YOURS WILL KEEP YOU FROM ME?
WAR?
YES, A LITTLE, BUT WARS HAVE ENDINGS.
THEY HAVE TWO, IN FACT. ONE HAPPY, THE OTHER LESS SO...
HUSH. I WILL WIN.
THANKS TO YOUR "PRECIOUS" WORK?
A GREAT WORK, YES. THE MOST BEAUTIFUL THERE IS. UNIQUE, POWERFUL, AND MYSTERIOUS.
PRECISELY.

I CAN'T UNDERSTAND THE EASE WITH WHICH EVERYONE BUYS INTO YOUR PROJECTS.

THE PROMINENT FAMILIES FOLLOW YOU, THE ULEMAS FOLLOW YOU...
YOUR HUSBAND AND HIS FATHER CREATED A LOT OF BITTERNESS.

THEY SURROUNDED THEMSELVES WITH EXPERTS CHOSEN SOLELY ON THEIR SKILLS AND COMPETENCE.
THEY DIDN'T CARE IF THEY WERE JEWS, SLAVES, EUNUCHS, CHRISTIANS, SAQALIBA... AS LONG AS THEY WERE BRILLIANT.

IT WAS CONSISTENT WITH THEIR IDEALS OF EXCELLENCE AND OPENNESS. BUT IT CREATED RESENTMENT.
THIS RESENTMENT HAS HAD FIFTY YEARS TO RIPEN. I'M MERELY HARVESTING THE FRUIT.

THE GREAT ARAB FAMILIES ARE DRUNK WITH POWER. THE IMAMS ARE STRIPPED OF THEIR AUTHORITY AND FURIOUS AT SEEING ALL THE WOMEN BEING EDUCATED IN THE COPYISTS' QUARTERS. I'M THEIR OPPORTUNE MAN. I'M REDISTRIBUTING THE ROLES.

MEN ARE PATHETIC.
LUCKY FOR US. I WAS BORN WITHOUT NOBILITY, YOU WERE BORN A SLAVE. AND LOOK AT US TODAY.
WE'RE DOING PRETTY WELL.

I SAY IT'S TOO RISKY. WE CAN'T LET ANYONE SEE US.
BUT THEY'VE GOT A DONKEY, LUBNA! WITH A SECOND ANIMAL, WE'D BE GOOD TO GO.
AND WHAT DO YOU WANT TO BUY THIS DONKEY WITH?
WHO SAYS WE'RE BUYING IT?
THERE'S NO WAY WE'RE STEALING THESE POOR PEOPLE'S DONKEY!!
BUT...
NO BUTS!
LOOK! IN THEIR BASKETS... THEY LOOK LIKE FIGS!
OH, FIG HEAVEN! LOTS OF FIGS!

PEACE BE WITH YOU, GOOD PEOPLE.
HAT DO WANT?!
STAY BACK! THIEF!
WE'RE NOT THIEVES, MA'AM, SIMPLY LOST TRAVELERS, AND WE... WE'RE STARVING!
WOULD YOU BE WILLING TO SELL US SOME FIGS?
DO YOU HAVE ENOUGH TO PAY?
N... NO. WE APPEAL TO YOUR CHARITY, MA'AM.
CHARITY?
DON'T LET THEM!

WE WORKED HARD TO PICK THOSE FIGS! WE BROKE OUR BACKS AND SLEPT OUTSIDE!
AND WE'RE GOING TO DRY THESE FIGS AND SELL THEM, BECAUSE THAT'S ALL WE HAVE TO LIVE ON.
I UNDERSTAND, MA'AM, BUT DOESN'T GOD SAY WE SHOULD HELP THE POOR AND--

YOU'RE POOR? **HA!** YOU SEEM WELL-FED FOR A PAUPER!

AND THIS... NEVER IN MY LIFE COULD I DREAM OF WEARING SUCH A FINE DRESS. LEAVE GOD'S WORD OUT OF THIS.

MADAM, I SEE YOU UNDERSTAND THE VALUE OF THINGS. TAKE A LOOK AT THIS.
WHAT... ?!?
THIS BOOK VERY OLD, A ITS COVER IS WITH SILVER RUBIES. ISN' MAGNIFICEN

ARE YOU CRAZY?! THAT'S A VOLUME OF IBN ABD RABBIH'S "THE UNIQUE NECKLACE"!
IT CERTAINLY IS VERY NICE...
RIGHT YOU ARE, MADAM. THIS IS A REAL TREASURE.

WELL, MADAM, THIS BOOK COULD BE YOURS IN EXCHANGE FOR YOUR DONKEY AND YOUR FIGS! AND YOU'D WIN THE DEAL, BECAUSE IT'S WORTH SO MUCH MORE!
HUH!! NOT AT ALL! DON'T LISTEN TO HIM! HE'S DELIRIOUS!

"THE UNIQUE NECKLACE" IS A SET OF 25 VOLUMES...
...ALL NAMED AFTER PRECIOUS STONES AND DECORATED ACCORDINGLY.

IT'S ABOUT KNOWLEDGE AND THE SCIENCES, AND THERE'S NO QUESTION OF--
SHHHT.
LET ME FINISH. DO YOU WANT TO EAT, YES OR NO?

I REMIND YOU THAT WE'RE TRYING TO SAVE THESE BOOKS!
WITH TWO BEASTS INSTEAD OF ONE, AND A FULL BELLY, WE'LL SAVE THEM ALL THE BETTER!
NO!
YES!

HEY... DON'T BOTHER. I'M NOT INTERESTED.

WHAT? BUT MADAM, THIS BOOK IS WORTH THE PRICE OF A HUNDRED DONKEYS, AND...
MAYBE SO, BUT I WOULDN'T KNOW WHO TO SELL IT TO. AND I'D BE ACCUSED OF STEALING IT. I'D GET IN TROUBLE.

YOU SELL IT, IF IT'S SO VALUABLE! AND THEN YOU CAN BUY ALL THE DONKEYS AND FIGS YOU WANT!

HAHA! YOUNG MAN... WHAT A SAGACIOUS MIND...

BUT THE VALUE OF A BOOK CANNOT BE REDUCED TO THE QUALITY OF ITS DECORATIONS. ABOVE ALL, IT'S A WORK OF ART. IT'S KNOWLEDGE. CAN YOU READ, SON?

WELL, NO. WHY WOULD I?

HERE'S WHAT I PROPOSE.

YOU'RE GOING TO CHOOSE A RANDOM PAGE FROM THIS BOOK, AND I'M GOING TO READ IT TO YOU. IF MY READING TEACHES YOU ANYTHING, YOU'LL GIVE US A FEW FIGS FROM YOUR BASKET...

WHAT DO YOU SAY? SPIRITUAL FOOD FOR EARTHLY FOOD...

PEUH! LEAVE IT, TEWFIK. THERE'S NOTHING BUT CHATTER IN THOSE THINGS, STUFF THAT'S USELESS TO THE REST OF US.
RECONSIDER, MA'AM. KNOWLEDGE IS USEFUL FOR EVERYONE.
ALRIGHT.

I CHOOSE THIS PAGE.

AH! YOU COULDN'T HAVE PICKED BETTER. IN THIS PASSAGE, IBN ABD RABBIH TALKS ABOUT ANAXIMANDER OF MILETUS. DO YOU KNOW WHO ANAXIMANDER WAS?
UH... NO...

HE WAS A GREEK PHILOSOPHER WHO LIVED OVER A THOUSAND YEARS AGO! A SAGE LIKE FEW OTHERS!

IT'S A PASSAGE THAT TALKS ABOUT THE ORIGINS OF LIFE. DO YOU KNOW ANYTHING ABOUT THE ORIGINS OF LIFE?
YEAH, IT'S GOD. HE CREATED THE WORLD AND LIFE. EVERYONE KNOWS THAT.
YES, BUT LET'S TAKE A LOOK AT WHAT ANAXIMANDER SAYS IN HIS GREAT WISDOM: "ANIMALS ARE BORN FROM THE MOISTURE EVAPORATED BY THE SUN." INTERESTING...
HMM... LET'S SEE WHAT HAPPENS NEXT: "...BUT MAN WAS BEGOTTEN BY ANOTHER ANIMAL, MORE PRECISELY THE FISH, AND IN THE BEGINNING, HE LOOKED LIKE A..."
GULP... "A FISH."
HAHAHA!

"IN THE BEGINNING, MAN LOOKED LIKE A FISH." GREAT.
WATCH YOUR TONE!
IS THAT WHY WE'RE RISKING OUR LIVES?!
FOR THIS KIND OF NONSENSE?!
IS THAT WHY THEY THREW ME IN THE GUADALQUIVIR?!
"IN THE BEGINNING, MAN LOOKED LIKE A FISH...
"...AND, IN THE END, HE WILL BE DEVOURED BY FISH, JUST LIKE POOR MARWAN!"
ANAXIMANDER WAS A GREAT THINKER!
IF HE SAYS THAT MAN LOOKED LIKE A FISH, MAYBE IT'S TRUE!
WHAT DO WE REALLY KNOW FOR SURE? SCIENCE DEMANDS THAT WE REJECT NO HYPOTHESIS OUTRIGHT!

THAT'S NOT A HYPOTHESIS, IT'S JUST STUPID! STUPID AND BLASPHEMOUS!
IT'S GOD WHO CREATED MAN! AND HE CREATED THEM ON THE EARTH! NOT IN THE SEA!

BECAUSE HE PUT FISH IN THE SEA! AND BIRDS IN THE SKY!
WHY WOULD YOU WANT IT ANY MORE COMPLICATED THAN THAT?!

A BABY IN IT MOTHER'S WOMB IS SURROUNDED BY LIQUID. IT LIVES THERE LIKE A FISH FOR NINE MONTHS...
ARG! YOU HAVE AN ANSWER FOR EVERYTHING!

THAT'S RIGHT! AND SINCE YOU'RE TALKING ABOUT BIRDS, YOU SHOULD KNOW THAT MAN CAN FLY, TOO!

HE'S CRAZY. THIS MAN IS CRAZY.

IT'S NOT ME WHO'S CRAZY...
IT'S ABBAS IBN FIRNAS, WHO LEAPT FROM THE TOP OF CÓRDOBA'S HIGHEST MINARET A HUNDRED YEARS AGO!

AND HE LANDED 70 METERS FROM SAID MINARET, THANKS TO A FLYING MACHINE OF HIS OWN INVENTION.
YOU'RE LYING.
NOT AT ALL! IT'S ALL DETAILED HERE, IN HIS HAND-WRITTEN ACCOUNT, WITH SCHEMATICS AND EVERYTHING.
HE REALLY FLEW? IN THE SKY?
WELL, HE GLIDED, BUT YOU HAVE TO START SOMEWHERE.
AND NOTHING BAD HAPPENED?
HE BROKE BOTH LEGS WHEN HE LANDED. BUT HE WAS AIRBORNE FOR MORE THAN A MINUTE! BEFORE SEVERAL WITNESSES! AND HE SURVIVED!
CRASH!

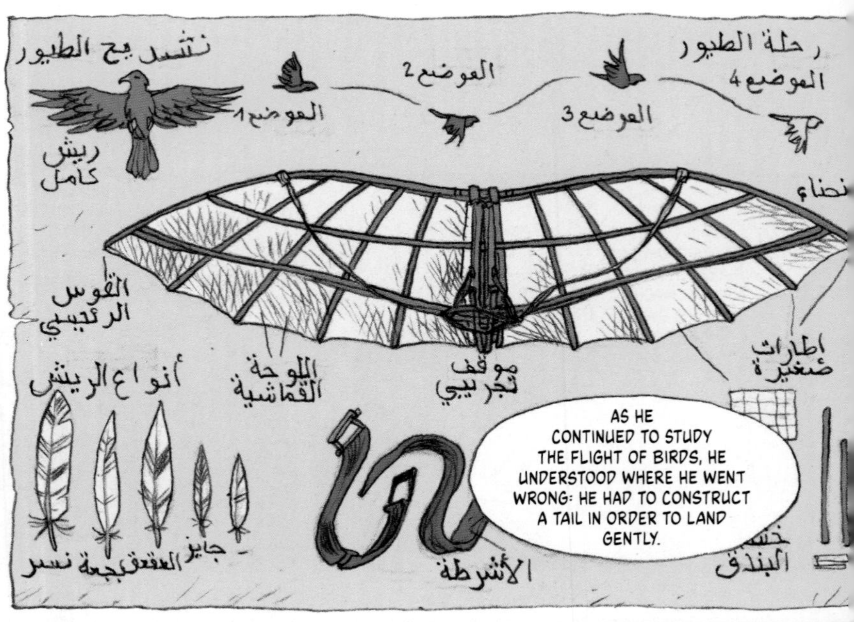

رحلة الطيور
ريش كامل
أنواع الريش
اللوحة القماشية
موقف تجريبي
إطارات صغيرة
الأشرطة
AS HE CONTINUED TO STUDY THE FLIGHT OF BIRDS, HE UNDERSTOOD WHERE HE WENT WRONG: HE HAD TO CONSTRUCT A TAIL IN ORDER TO LAND GENTLY.

BY THAT TIME, HOWEVER, IT WAS TOO LATE FOR HIM. HE WAS ALREADY 62 YEARS OLD.
BUT... I... JEEZ...

IN ANY CASE, WE'RE STILL RUNNING ON EMPTY STOMACHS.
AND TWO CARELESS PEOPLE HAVE SHOWN A PRICELESS BOOK TO AN OLD PEASANT WOMAN...

I'D GIVE ANYTHING FOR A FIG.

WHAT?!? HOW...?!?

SHHHH!

GULP.
RAAAAAAAAH
WHAT'S WRONG NOW?
WAIT... LET ME THINK...
I'M SURE I HAVE IT SOMEWHERE...
WHAT?
HERE! THE "CHRONICLES OF CÓRDOBA"!
WAIT HERE. I'LL BE BACK!

HEY!
WAIT! WAIT!
GIVE ME ONE MORE CHANCE

ARE YOU...
HUFF.
HUFF.
...A GOOD MUSLIM, CHILD?
OF COURSE I'M A GOOD MUSLIM!

AND DID YOU KNOW THAT, IF YOU'RE A MUSLIM HERE, UNDER THE PROTECTION OF THE CALIPHS OF AL-ANDALUS, IT'S BECAUSE OF A FIG?

HUH?!

IT WAS ALMOST 300 YEARS AGO...

At that time, what was to become Al-Andalus was a Visigoth land.
The Visigoths were Arian Christians. Above all, they were warriors. Prowess was no joke among the Visigoths. Córdoba was one of their strongholds.
Nothing could threaten their power.
And yet...

One day, 700 Muslim riders crossed the sea for the first time near Algeciras...
...And arrived at the foot of Córdoba's walls. Their leader was called Mughith al-Rumi. They pitched their tents on the opposite bank of the Guadalquivir and waited patiently for something to happen.
Within the city, the Visigoths were not concerned. Their walls were high, and they had enough to withstand a long siege.
Despite their bravery, Mughith al-Rumi's horsemen could not make a move...
But then... the unexpected happened.

The civilian population didn't much like the Visigoths. The Muslim warriors were informed by a shepherd that, somewhere alongside the wall, a breach in was accessible to an agile man.
And so, one night...
The breach was high up, inaccessible from the ground. Just below it, however.... A majestic fig tree had grown...

The most agile of the men climbed the tree, and from there...

The next day, they were masters of the city. Cōrdoba became the first Muslim stronghold in the land that would become Al-Andalus.
ALL THANKS TO A FIG THAT FELL AT THE FOOT OF THE RAMPARTS!
OUAAAAH! AMAZING! GOD IS GREAT!
TAKE THAT, YOU FILTHY VISIGOTH! YAAAAAAH!
I AM MUGHITH AL-RUMI!
I'D NEVER HEARD THAT BEFORE.
IT'S A WONDERFUL STORY.

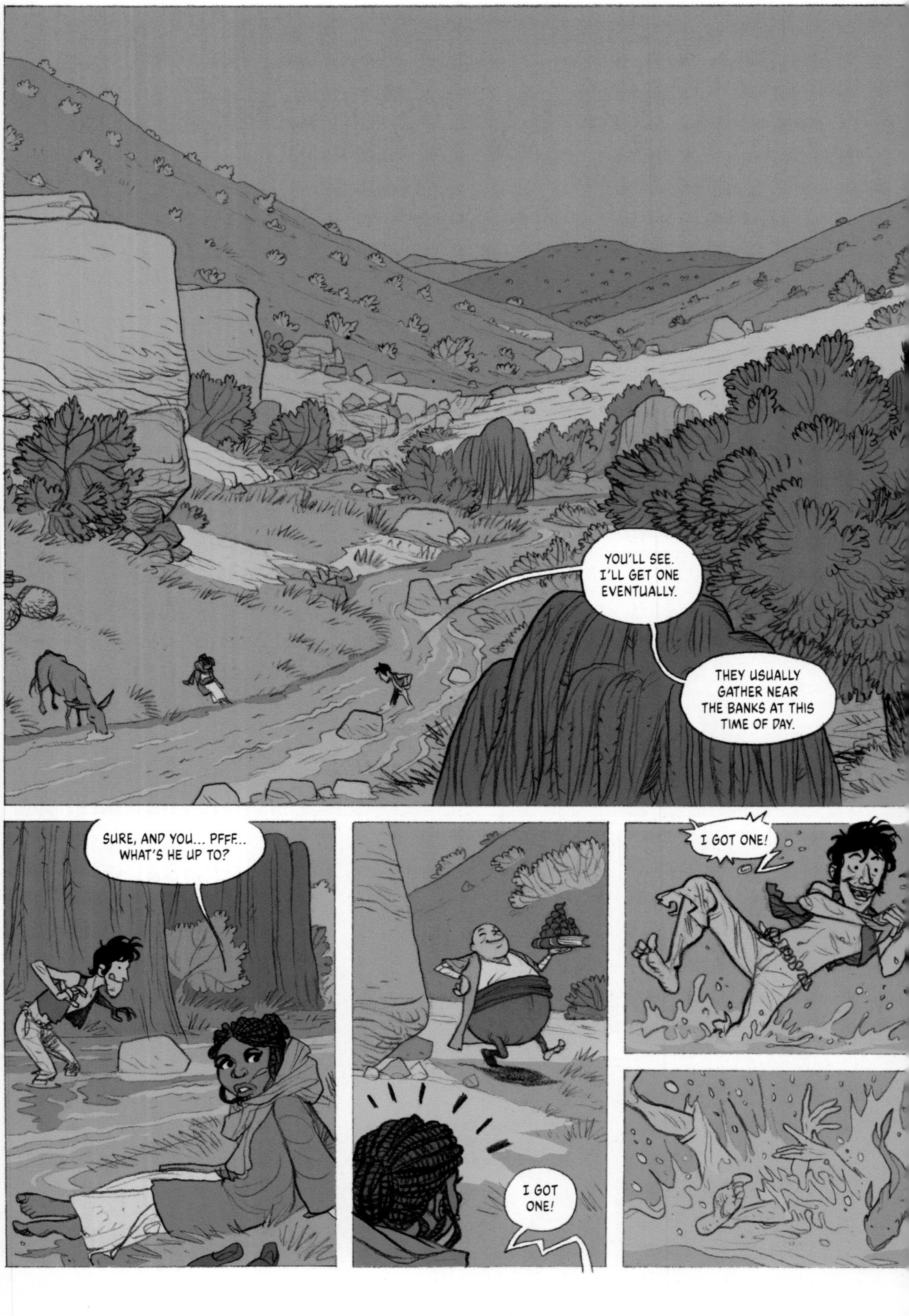

YOU'LL SEE. I'LL GET ONE EVENTUALLY.

THEY USUALLY GATHER NEAR THE BANKS AT THIS TIME OF DAY.

SURE, AND YOU... PFFF.. WHAT'S HE UP TO?

I GOT ONE!

I GOT ONE!

THEY'RE DELICIOUS, THESE FIGS.
IT MUST BE RECOGNIZED.

MNFF.

OF COURSE, FISH OR CHICKEN WOULD HAVE BEEN WONDERFUL, TOO, BUT...

FORTUNATELY, WE HAVE MY FIGS, WON HONESTLY, THANKS TO A BEAUTIFUL STORY FOUND IN THESE BEAUTIFUL BOOKS.
BLAH, BLAH, BLAH. WE GET IT.

DON'T BE A SORE LOSER, MARWAN.
I'M GOING TO SLEEP. GOOD NIGHT.

WELL,
PRETTY GAZELLE?

HEHEH... BEAUTIFUL MORNING, ISN'T IT?
IMBECILE. WHAT'S WRONG WITH YOU?

YOU SCARED ME! THIS IS INAPPROPRIATE. TURN AROUND.
OH, IT'S FINE.

SPLASH

FOR ONCE, THAT GRUMP TARID ISN'T ON OUR BACKS. WE CAN HAVE A LITTLE FUN.

WHAT'S "A LITTLE FUN," EXACTLY?
YOU KNOW... AND I'M SURE YOU LIKE ME A LITTLE BIT.

OH, ENORMOUSLY. IGNORANT, SNEAKY CLODS... THAT'S WHAT I LIKE.
AH, OF COURSE. I'M NOT A SCHOLAR OF MANNERS.

I'M NOT THE CAAAALIPH ABD AL-RAHMAN III, WHO APPEALED SO MUCH TO WOMEN WITH HIS LOOOONG, FRAGRANT, BLOND HAIR AND KOHL-RINGED, BLUE EYES.
THAT'S THE KIND OF MAN YOU LIKE, ISN'T IT? ERUDITE AND REFINED?

ABD AL-RAHMAN III WAS A GREAT SCHOLAR, POET, AND STATESMAN...
BLAHBLAHBLAH...

...BUT HE WAS ALSO A MAN OF POWER. HE THREW AWAY THOUSANDS OF SUBLIME SLAVES WORKING IN HIS SERVICE, EACH ON A WHIM.

ONE DAY, ONE OF THEM REFUSED TO LET HIM KISS HER, BECAUSE HE REEKED OF GARLIC AND ALCOHOL.

URNED HER FACE WITH A TORCH SO THAT
O ONE WOULD EVER WANT HER AGAIN.

MY FAVORED MAN, MARWAN, IS A KIND MAN, AND I HAVE NEVER MET ONE. EXCEPT TARID, WHO IS, INCIDENTALLY, A EUNUCH.

TURN AROUND. I'M GETTING OUT.

I **AM** KIND, I'LL HAVE YOU KNOW!
STAY IN THE COLD WATER FOR A WHILE. IT'LL CALM YOU DOWN.

AH!
THERE YOU ARE.

WHERE HAVE YOU BEEN? YOU THINK I SHOULD LOAD EVERYTHING BY MYSELF?
DON'T WORRY, WE'LL HELP YOU.

WHA... WHAT ARE YOU DOING?

YOU CAN SEE WHAT WE'RE DOING. WE'RE ROBBING YOU. WE'VE HEARD ABOUT YOUR BOOK SET WITH STONES AND SILVER, BUT THIS...

THIS IS BEYOND ANYTHING WE IMAGINED.
THERE YOU ARE. YOU AND YOUR FIGS...

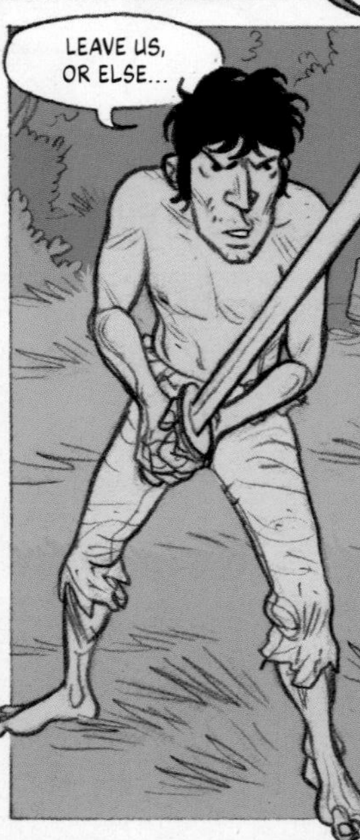
LEAVE US, OR ELSE...

OR ELSE WHAT, KID? DON'T BE AN IDIOT. YOU DON'T LOOK LIKE A WARRIOR.
YOU'RE LUCKY WE'RE NOT HANDING YOU OVER TO THE SOLDIERS.
I HEAR THERE ARE PATROLS OUT LOOKING FOR RUNAWAY SLAVES.

YOU... YOU DON'T KNOW WHAT YOU'RE DOING! THESE BOOKS ARE PRICELESS!
THAT'S EXACTLY WHY WE'RE TAKING THEM. HAHAHA!

BUT IT'S YOURSELF YOU'RE ROBBING! IT'S YOUR HERITAGE! YOUR CULTURE! THEY'RE DESTROYING OUR CULTURE OVER THERE IN CÓRDOBA! AND YOU'RE STEALING WHAT'S LEFT!
COME BACK!

WHAT'S HE SAYING?
CITY GIBBERISH. DON'T WORRY ABOUT IT.

GIVE ME THAT SWORD! I HAVE TO DO SOMETHING!
YOU'RE NOT SERIOUS...

I AM. THERE'S NO OTHER OPTION...
UH, TARID, WHAT ARE YOU...?

TARID! NO!

THIS MULE'S A PIECE OF WORK. DON'T THINK I'VE SEEN A WORSE ONE BEFORE.
YAAAAAAH!

HEY! WATCH IT!

HUUUUUUN!

TARID!

TARID, NO!

A WORD OF ADVICE: TRY TO BE A LITTLE LESS STUPID THAN YOUR FRIEND.

WHAT SHOULD WE DO? GOD, TARID, DON'T DIE. PLEASE DON'T DIE!
RAAAAAH...

RAAAAAHHHHZIIIII!
WHAT?
RAAAZI...
WHAT'S HE SAYING?

HE'S SAYING "RAZI." WE HAVE ONE OF HIS MEDICAL TREATISES. ON THE MULE. "FOR ONE WHO HAS NO PHYSICIAN TO ATTEND HIM."
WE...WE DON'T HAVE THE MULE ANYMORE.
IT'S FINE. I'VE COPIED THAT BOOK EIGHT TIMES.

KEEP HOLDING THE WOUND! IT'LL SLOW THE BLOOD LOSS. I'LL TRY TO FIND SOME HELP.

BUT... LUBNA! WAIT! DON'T LEAVE ME LIKE THIS...
I'LL BE BACK!

PRESS HARD TO STOP THE BLOOD FLOWING.

HEY!
WHAT'S THE PROBLEM NOW?!

AOUCH!

SHE HURT ME, THAT FILTH!

I'LL SHOW YOU...!!
LEAVE HER BE. SHE'S A HALF-DEAD OLD BEAST.

WHAT ARE WE GOING TO DO WITH THESE BOOKS? WE CAN'T CARRY THEM OURSELVES!
AND THEY DON'T FIT ON THE MULE.

WE WON'T HAVE TO CARRY THEM. I HAVE AN IDEA.

THE INFERNO'S FINALLY DYING. I THOUGHT IT WOULD NEVER HAPPEN. IT'S BEEN BURNING FOR ALMOST A WEEK NOW.
YESTERDAY, THOSE FOOLS REVIVED IT WITH A GRAND CONTRIBUTION FROM RAZI.
WHO'S RAZI?
A SERVANT OF SATAN FROM PERSIA!
HE REJECTS THE EXISTENCE OF GOD AND CALLS HIM A TYRANT. HE ADVOCATES FOR DEMOCRACY AND SAYS WE SHOULD STOP EATING ANIMALS.
HE'S A FREE THINKER AND A BLASPHEMER! IT WAS URGENT TO BURN IT ALL TO ASH!
YES, BUT HE WAS ALSO VERY KNOWLEDGEABLE. MEDICINE OWES HIM A GREAT DEBT. AND THE COPY OF HIS "DIVINE SCIENCES" THAT WE BURNED WAS A MARVEL...
THE ANATOMICAL DRAWINGS WERE--
REGRETS, GRAND VIZIER?
I'M NO LONGER DIRECTLY SUPERVISING, BUT I DID REQUEST THAT IT BE SPARED FOR MY PERSONAL LIBRARY.
YOUR SERVANTS ARE ZEALOUS.
WE'RE READY TO GO, O VIZIER.
AH! AT LAST!
IT'S HIGH TIME TO LEAVE. WE CAN'T HOLD THE BERBER TRIBES ANY LONGER. COMPLAINTS ARE POURING IN FROM EVERYWHERE.

THEY'RE CONDUCTING RAIDS ACROSS THE COUNTRYSIDE. WHOLE VILLAGES...
THEY BEHAVE LIKE SAVAGES.
"God divided anger into ten, and he gave nine-tenths to the Berbers, distributing the rest among the peoples of the earth."
THEY'RE BORED. I'LL GIVE THEM SOMETHING TO DO.
YES. IT'S TIME TO BRING THEM WAR.
YOU OWE US WAR, AS WELL, AMIR. WE BLESS YOUR POLICIES, AND YOU'VE PROMISED A REVIVAL OF HOLY WAR IN EXCHANGE.
I'M WORKING ON IT.
IT'S ALL GOING TO END BADLY.
IT'LL ALL WORK OUT IN THE END.
BERBERS ARE THE BEST MERCENARIES.
THEIR PRESENCE WEAKENS THE ARAB DYNASTIES THAT CHALLENGE ME. THANKS TO THE BERBERS, TO BLACK SLAVES AND CHRISTIAN MERCENARIES, I NO LONGER DEPEND ON THEM.
WE'RE GOING TO ENSLAVE THE CHRISTIAN KINGDOMS OF SPAIN, DESTROY THEM.
CÓRDOBA WILL BE OVER-FLOWING WITH TREASURE, FOOD, AND SLAVES.
WE'LL LIVE IN OPULENCE. AND WAR WILL BE FAR FROM OUR FLOWERING GARDENS.

YOU FAILED IN YOUR MISSION, YAKUB. BECAUSE OF YOU, I'M GOING TO WAR WITHOUT MY SECRET WEAPON.

IF I MAY, GRAND VIZIER...
IT'S NOT ENTIRELY MY FAULT. WHAT YOU COVET WOULD ALREADY BE YOURS IF JEWS WERE TREATED BETTER IN AL-ANDALUS.
WE TREAT JEWS VERY WELL.

BETTER THAN ANYWHERE ELSE IN THE WORLD. YOU WORSHIP FREELY, YOU TRADE, YOU PROSPER... WHAT ARE YOU COMPLAINING ABOUT?
WE ARE OVERTAXED, CERTAIN PROFESSIONS AND PUBLIC OFFICES ARE FORBIDDEN TO US...

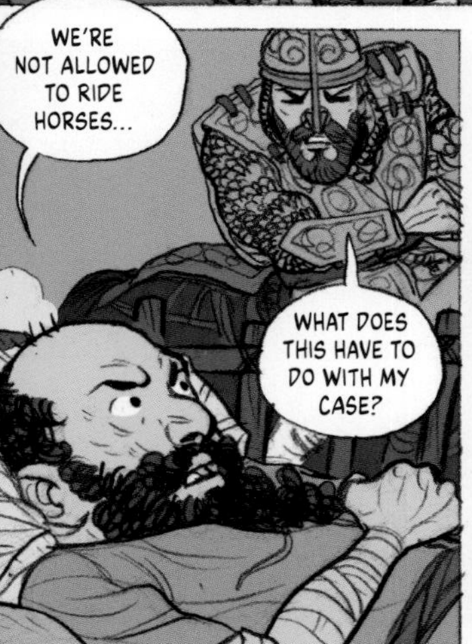

WE'RE NOT ALLOWED TO RIDE HORSES...
WHAT DOES THIS HAVE TO DO WITH MY CASE?

MY POINT, GRAND VIZIER, IS THAT, IF I HADN'T BEEN OBLIGED TO TRAVEL FROM SEVILLE TO CÓRDOBA ON A STUPID MULE THAT THREW ME FROM A PRECIPICE...
...YOUR CASE WOULD HAVE BEEN SETTLED LONG AGO.

MMMMHH... CERTAINLY.

RSTL

COME ON!

TARID! COME ON!

HE'S TOO SOFT, THIS KID!

A WUSS! A TOTAL WUSS!

THERE'S NO PLACE FOR WEAK PEOPLE IN THIS WORLD, KID!

NO ROOM!

START AGAIN!

RECITE!

RECITE!

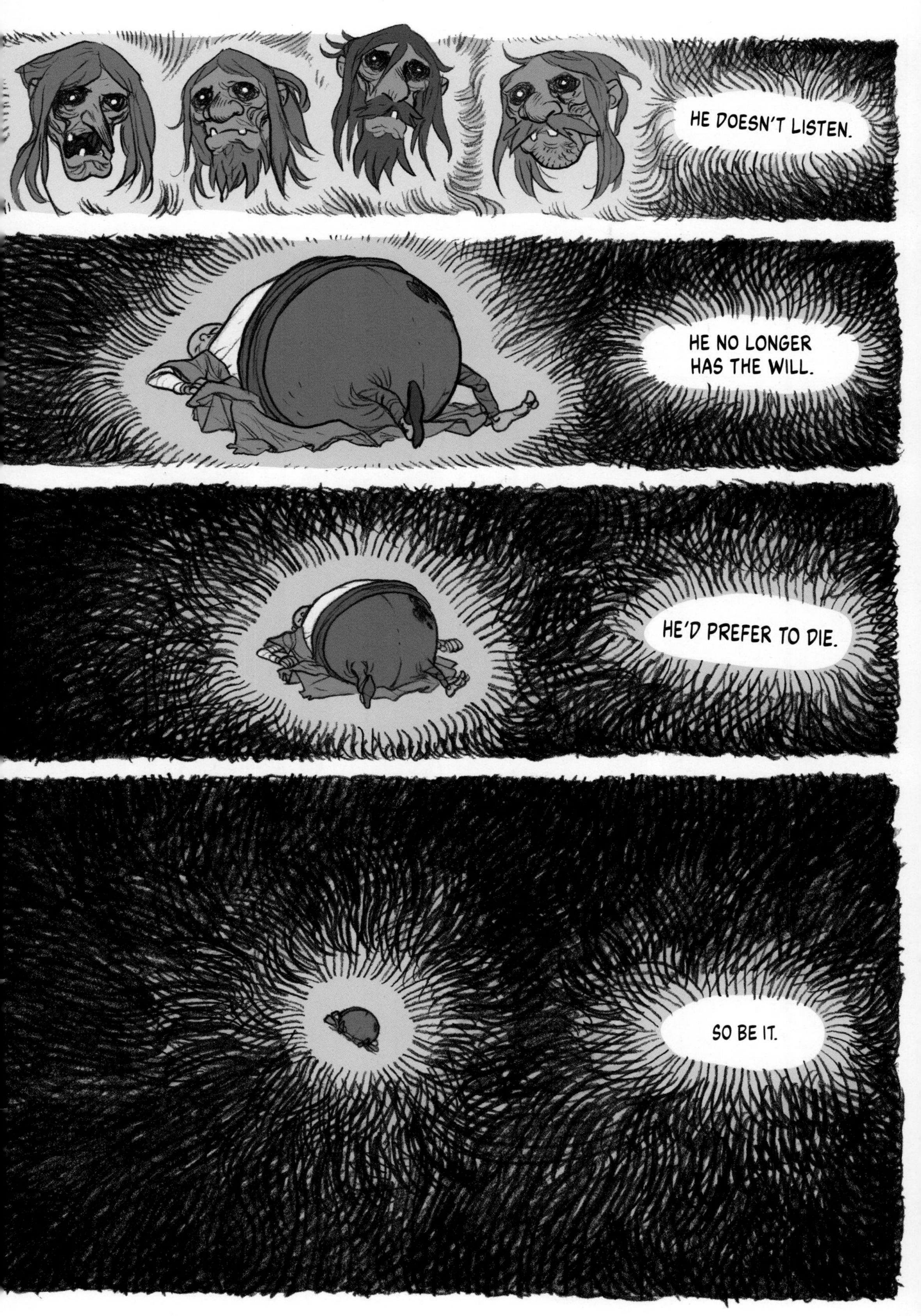
HE DOESN'T LISTEN.
HE NO LONGER HAS THE WILL.
HE'D PREFER TO DIE.
SO BE IT.

MARWAN!
HOW IS HE?
STILL WARM.
WHAT HAPPENED
TO YOU?

I FOUND WHAT RAZI PRESCRIBES FOR OPEN WOUNDS.

HONEY FOR THE WOUND.

CLAY TO PROTECT IT.

ROMAN CHAMOMILE TO FIGHT INFECTION...
...WHICH MUST BE BREWED.

AND PLANTAIN. I FOUND THE CLAY AT THE BOTTOM OF A RAVINE.
THE HONEY... WASN'T SO EASY.
LUBNA...

THERE.
NOW WE WAIT.

HAAAAAAA!

HEHEHE.

WHAT...?!?

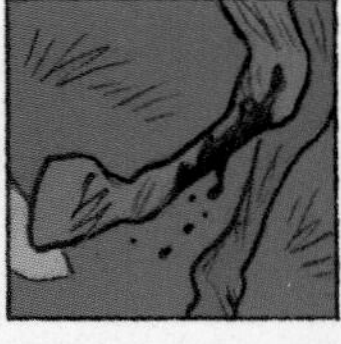

LUBNA!

GIVE HER THE REMAINING CHAMOMILE. IF IT'S GOOD FOR MEN, IT MUST BE GOOD FOR ANIMALS!
BUT TARID NEEDS IT...

HE NO LONGER HAS A FEVER.

THE CLAY PLASTER WILL AT LEAST PREVENT FLIES FROM LAYING EGGS IN THE WOUND.

THE CARGO WAS NOWHERE TO BE SEEN.

THERE IS NO MORE CARGO. WE NO LONGER HAVE REASON TO RUN. WE'VE LOST.
ALL THAT MATTERS NOW IS FINDING A DOCTOR FOR TARID AND A PLACE TO REST.
WE'LL WALK TO THE NEAREST VILLAGE AND ASK FOR THEIR HOSPITALITY.
WE CAN FIND A WAY TO MAKE OURSELVES USEFUL AND EARN A FEW DIRHEMS.
AS FOR YOU... I KNOW VERY WELL WHY YOU'VE COME BACK!
YOU ACT REBELLIOUS, BUT THE REALITY IS THAT, WITHOUT HUMANS, YOU'D BE DONE FOR! FROM NOW ON, IF YOU WANT TO STAY, IT'S GIVE AND TAKE!
NO MORE BAD WILL!
YOU... YOU'RE NEGOTIATING WITH A MULE, MARWAN.
THERE'S NO NEGOTIATION!

CAN I SAY SOMETHING?
GO AHEAD.
WHAT'S JUST HAPPENED IS EXACTLY WHAT I THOUGHT THE WORLD WAS LIKE BEFORE I MET YOU.
MEANING?
MEANING THAT, DEEP DOWN, PEOPLE DON'T CARE ABOUT CULTURE, SCIENCE, PHILOSOPHY, OR ANYTHING ELSE THAT HAPPENED IN THAT LIBRARY OF YOURS.
THE OLD LADY AND THE BOY DIDN'T WANT TO EXCHANGE A SINGLE FIG FOR THAT PRECIOUS VOLUME BECAUSE, DEEP DOWN, THEY DON'T CARE.
THOSE PEASANTS HAVE NO INTENTION OF READING A SINGLE LINE OF WHAT THEY STOLE FROM US. THEY DON'T CARE AT ALL, ANAXIMANDER OR RABBIH.
WE'RE RISKING OUR LIVES FOR NOTHING BECAUSE, DEEP DOWN, ALL PEOPLE WANT IS TO BE RICH.
I THINK YOU'RE WRONG.
OH, YEAH?
YEAH.

THE SO-CALLED "FREE" MEN AND WOMEN THAT WE'VE MET ACTUALLY SPEND THEIR LIVES BEING AFRAID.
AFRAID OF BEING HUNGRY OR COLD, AFRAID OF BEING ROBBED OR KILLED BY RAIDERS, A CAPRICIOUS LORD, OR AN ARMY ON THE MARCH. THEIR THOUGHTS ARE OCCUPIED WITH FEAR.
FEAR OF TOMORROW, FEAR OF THE NEXT DAY, FEAR OF OTHERS.

TO BE ABLE TO THINK, THE MIND MUST BE FREE AND AT PEACE.

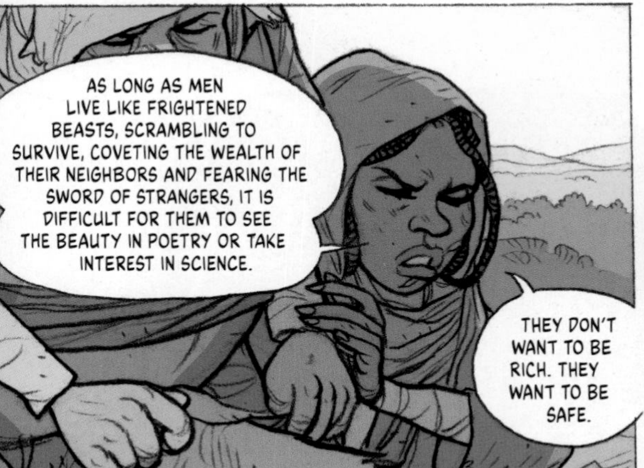
AS LONG AS MEN LIVE LIKE FRIGHTENED BEASTS, SCRAMBLING TO SURVIVE, COVETING THE WEALTH OF THEIR NEIGHBORS AND FEARING THE SWORD OF STRANGERS, IT IS DIFFICULT FOR THEM TO SEE THE BEAUTY IN POETRY OR TAKE INTEREST IN SCIENCE.
THEY DON'T WANT TO BE RICH. THEY WANT TO BE SAFE.

AND WEALTH ALLOWS FOR RESPITE.
TARID AND I ARE SLAVES, IT'S TRUE, BUT WE ARE LUCKY TO BE HIGH-RANKED, EDUCATED SLAVES.

MANY THINGS WERE FORBIDDEN TO US, BUT WE LIVED WITHOUT FEAR AND IN SECURITY, WITH A SINGLE MISSION: TO DEVELOP, PROTECT, AND CHERISH THE LIBRARY OF CÓRDOBA.
THE GREEK PHILOSOPHERS DID NOT WORK THE FIELDS. NEITHER DID ABD AL-RAHMAN III.
SO, OF COURSE--
LUBNA...

HAHAHA!
THOSE FOOLS! THEY LEFT THE PAGES, MARWAN!
THEY TOOK THE BINDINGS AND LEFT THE PAGES!

HAHAHA! EVERYTHING'S HERE, MARWAN!

EVERYTHING'S HERE! LOOK!

THE BOOKS! GOD IS GREAT!

OOOOAHHH! OUCH!
TARID!

OUCH!

I THINK YOU BROKE YOUR SHOULDER WHEN YOU FELL, TARID.
JUST MY LUCK.

WHAT'S WITH YOU? YOU WENT FROM DYING TO EXALTED IN A SECOND.
HAVEN'T YOU BEEN PAYING ATTENTION, MARWAN?
THESE WORKS HAVE ESCAPED FIRE, RAIN, FALLS INTO RAVINES, AND NOW THEY'VE BEEN SKINNED!
BUT THEY'RE STILL HERE.
AND SO ARE WE.

YES, SO ARE WE.
TARID, YOU TALKED A LOT IN YOUR DELIRIUM. YOU SPOKE TO PEOPLE...
"BROTHERS," YOU SAID... BROTHER ANTONIUS, BROTHER GREGORY...

OH... REALLY?
YES. YOU RECITED LATIN, TOO. WHERE ARE YOU FROM, TARID?

FROM THE DARKNESS...

I DON'T KNOW WHERE I AM.
PROBABLY FAR TO THE NORTH, SOMEWHERE IN WEST FRANCIA OR LOTHARINGIA.
NO MATTER.
I HAVE NO MEMORY OF ANY OF THAT.

ALL I KNOW IS THAT, AS A CHILD, I WAS FOUND IN THE SNOW BY A GROUP OF BEGGING MONKS.
THEY WERE FOUR OLD COPYISTS, BLINDED BY A LIFE SPENT IN THE DARKNESS OF THE WORKROOM.
THEIR ABBEY HAD BEEN DESTROYED BY THE NORMANS. CONDEMNED TO WANDERING, THEY LIVED ON CHARITY.

I WAS SOON ABLE TO
MANAGE ON MY OWN.

I BECAME ESSENTIAL TO THEIR
LIVES. I BECAME THEIR EYES.

I GUIDED THEM TO THE
BEST PLACES TO BEG.

WITH THE ALMS MONEY, I BOUGHT GOOD
PRODUCTS, NEGOTIATED FOR THEM.

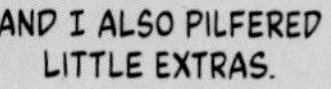

AND I ALSO PILFERED
LITTLE EXTRAS.

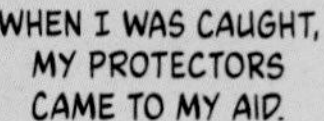

WHEN I WAS CAUGHT,
MY PROTECTORS
CAME TO MY AID.

WHEN I WASN'T BEING THEIR
GUIDE, I HAD TO STUDY.

MY PROTECTORS FORCED ME
TO LEARN THE BIBLE, LATIN,
AND GREEK EVERY DAY.

HUH?
BUT YOU
JUST SAID
THEY WERE
BLIND.

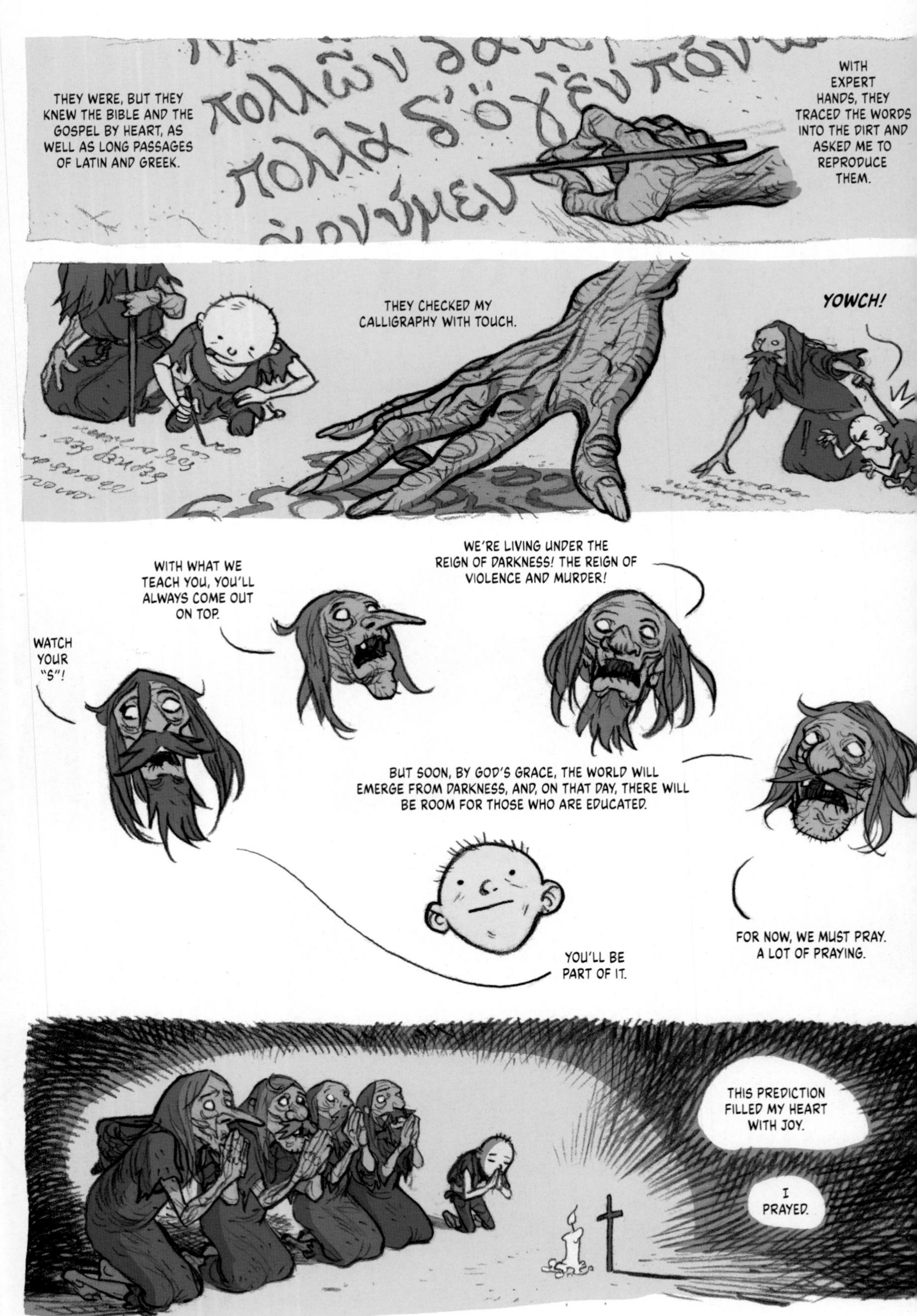
THEY WERE, BUT THEY KNEW THE BIBLE AND THE GOSPEL BY HEART, AS WELL AS LONG PASSAGES OF LATIN AND GREEK.
WITH EXPERT HANDS, THEY TRACED THE WORDS INTO THE DIRT AND ASKED ME TO REPRODUCE THEM.
THEY CHECKED MY CALLIGRAPHY WITH TOUCH.
YOWCH!
WITH WHAT WE TEACH YOU, YOU'LL ALWAYS COME OUT ON TOP.
WE'RE LIVING UNDER THE REIGN OF DARKNESS! THE REIGN OF VIOLENCE AND MURDER!
WATCH YOUR "S"!
BUT SOON, BY GOD'S GRACE, THE WORLD WILL EMERGE FROM DARKNESS, AND, ON THAT DAY, THERE WILL BE ROOM FOR THOSE WHO ARE EDUCATED.
YOU'LL BE PART OF IT.
FOR NOW, WE MUST PRAY. A LOT OF PRAYING.
THIS PREDICTION FILLED MY HEART WITH JOY.
I PRAYED.

I WORKED HARD.
I TAUGHT MYSELF TO USE A PEN.
I RECITED MY LATIN.
I PRAYED.
WHAT DO YOU WANT, DEAR MONKS? WE CAN'T WELCOME YOU. WE'RE TOO POOR.
READ THIS TEXT TO US, WON'T YOU?
"IN PRINCIPIO SEAVIT DEUS CAELUM ET TERRAM. TERRA AUTEMERAT INAMS ET VACUA, ET TENEBRAE ERANT SUPER FACIEM ABYSSI : ET SPIRITUS DEI FESEBATUR SU PER AQUAS DISITQUE DEUS : FIAT LUX. ET FACTA LUC."
WHAT DO YOU THINK? IS IT WELL WRITTEN?
NOT REALLY, NO. IT'S FULL OF SCRIBBLES, AND EVERY "S" IS NEARLY ILLEGIBLE.
YOU GOOD-FOR-NOTHING. THE "S"! THE "S" AGAIN!
SKAMP!
BUT-- AHH! BUT-- OOOOUCH!
THE WORLD WAS SLOW TO EMERGE FROM DARKNESS.

THE WORLD... WILL EMERGE... FROM THE DARKNESS. LEARN YOUR LATIN WELL. TAKE CARE OF YOUR "S"...
DON'T NEGLECT YOUR...
GREEK. I KNOW ALL ABOUT IT, BROTHER ANTONIUS. DON'T TIRE YOURSELF OUT.
LEFT TO MY OWN DEVICES, IN THOSE BARBARIC LANDS CONSTANTLY RAVAGED BY WAR, I COULDN'T BRING MYSELF TO ENTER HOLY ORDERS, THE ONLY REASONABLE WAY OUT OF MY SITUATION.

IN AN ABBEY, I WOULD'VE FOUND REFUGE AND PROBABLY SOME BREAD...
...BUT SOMETHING HELD ME BACK. DEEP DOWN, I LACKED FAITH. DESPITE THE TEACHINGS I'D RECEIVED. DESPITE THE PRAYERS.
SOME TIME LATER, I WAS CAUGHT STEALING. I WAS TEN YEARS OLD. AT FIRST, THEY THOUGHT OF HANGING ME.
THEN I POINTED OUT THAT I KNEW LATIN AND GREEK.
I WAS SENT TO VERDUN, WHERE I WAS SOLD INTO SLAVERY.

THERE, I WAS CASTRATED BY DOCTORS WHO OPERATED ON DOZENS OF CHILDREN EVERY DAY, TO FEED THE SLAVE TRADE BOUND FOR THE MEDITERRANEAN AND THE MUSLIM KINGDOMS.
HALF OF THE CHILDREN DID NOT SURVIVE THE OPERATION.
I SURVIVED ONCE AGAIN.
AND I PRAYED EVEN MORE.

VIA THE RHONE VALLEY, I WAS TRANSFERRED TO THE MUSLIM PORT OF FARAKHSHANIT,* WHERE I WAS ASSESSED.
I HAD BECOME A HEALTHY YOUNG EUNUCH. I KNEW LATIN AND GREEK.
I WAS TAUGHT ARABIC TO TRIPLE MY VALUE.

AT THE AGE OF ELEVEN, I WAS SENT TO CÓRDOBA.

ON THE BOAT, I WENT THROUGH HELL. I WAS SICK TO DEATH. I COULD SEE NO WAY OUT OF MY MISFORTUNE...

AND THEN I ARRIVED IN CÓRDOBA.
I DISCOVERED A WORLD I'D NEVER IMAGINED.
I WAS ASSIGNED TO THE COPYIST DEPARTMENT OF THE GREAT LIBRARY.

I WAS ADVISED TO CONVERT TO ISLAM, WHICH I GLADLY DID, SO THAT I COULD SHARE THE COPYISTS' MEALS.

I BECAME TARID.

**BAY OF SAINT-TROPEZ

I BEGAN TO EAT, EAT, EAT. I WAS NO LONGER COLD, NEVER HUNGRY, EVERYTHING WAS BEAUTIFUL.
THE LIGHT THAT BROTHER ANTONIUS SPOKE OF ILLUMINATED EVERYTHING.

YOU WERE A CHRISTIAN? BAPTIZED?
YES.

AND YOU DENIED YOUR FAITH FOR ISLAM?
YES. AND ALSO FOR CAKES.
CHRISTIANITY, ISLAM... ARE THEY TRULY SO DIFFERENT?

WELL, I WOULD SAY THAT... MY FAITH...
AS LONG AS WE'RE PRAYING FOR SOMETHING TO FALL FROM THE SKY...

...IT SEEMS WISER TO PRAY WITH OPEN HANDS...

...THAN WITH CLOSED HANDS.

AND THIS IS THE WORLD IN WHICH YOU HOPE TO SAVE THESE BOOKS?

WE DON'T HAVE MUCH FURTHER TO GO. TOMORROW, WITH A BIT OF LUCK, WE'LL REACH THE TAGUS.
AND ONCE WE'VE CROSSED IT, WE'LL SOON BE ON CHRISTIAN SOIL...

DON'T COMPLAIN. WITHOUT THE BINDINGS, IRON, AND JEWELRY, IT'S MUCH LIGHTER THAN BEFORE. WE SHOULD HAVE STARTED LIKE THIS.

WE WERE STUPID TO PUT ALL THAT ON THIS POOR BEAST.

OUR RESPECT FOR BOOKS HAS BLINDED US.

DO YOU REALLY THINK YOU'LL BE ABLE TO WALK?

I'LL BE FINE. I'M MORE WORRIED ABOUT HER.

THE TAGUS!
HA HA HAAAA!
WE MADE IT!

HIDE!

*ARABIC NAME FOR THE VIKINGS AT THIS TIME

YOU DON'T BELIEVE IN THE POWERS OF MADJUS, YET EVERYONE WHO'S COME ACROSS THEM SAYS THEY--
ABD AL-RAHMAN II DEFEATED THEM, REMEMBER?
HE TOOK BACK SEVILLE.
YEAH, BUT THAT DOESN'T MEAN...
COME ON, CHEER UP... WE'LL TRY TO CROSS FURTHER ON.
OH, NO!

HURRY! TURN AROUND!
AND GO WHERE?!
TO THE MADJUS!
HUH?! ARE YOU CRAZY?
THEY WANT TO KILL US! THE MADJUS, AT LEAST, MAY TAKE US ALIVE! LET'S GO!

COME ON! **COME ON!**

JUST LEAVE HER! IT'S TOO LATE FOR THE BOOKS ANYWAY!

NEVER!

WE CAN'T GIVE UP! NOT WHEN WE'RE SO CLOSE TO OUR GOAL!

OPEN YOUR EYES! IT'S ALL OVER! WE CAN ONLY SAVE OUR LIVES!

GOD CURSE IT! GET OUT OF THE WAY!

HERE. TRY THIS, MY DEAR. IT'S THE GREAT AL-KHWARIZMI. YOUR FAVORITE...

LET'S GO! KEEP MOVING! I'VE GOT SOME YUM-YUM FOR THE MULEY-MULE!

FORGIVE ME, AL-KHWARIZMI.

COME ON, MOVE!

TSSSST! THERE YOU GO!
IT'S VEEEEERY GOOD, AL-KHWARIZMI!

OW!
HOLD ON TO ME...

THEY'RE COMING!

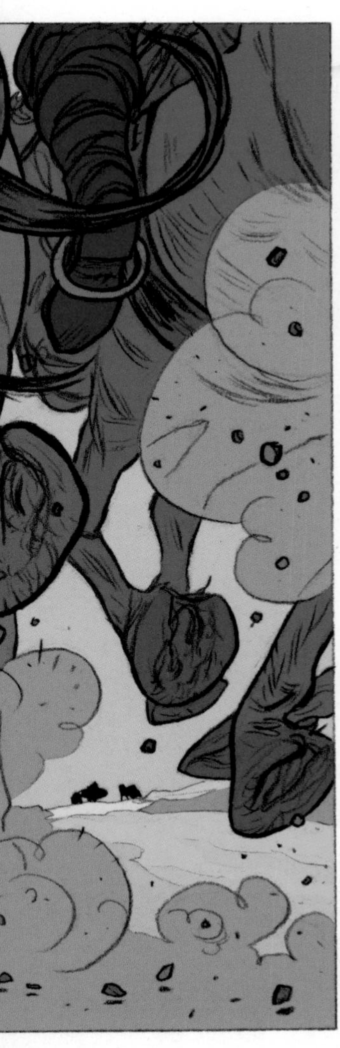

HEYYYYYYYYYY! EYYYHOOOOOO! MADJUS!

YOU GREAT BUNCH OF FILTH, CRAWLING WITH LICE! WE'RE HEEEEEEERE!

PEACE BE UPON YOU, SOLDIERS. WE DON'T WANT ANY TROUBLE.
WE'RE ON A MISSION FROM THE CALIPH OF CÓRDOBA, HISHAM II, COMMANDER OF THE FAITHFUL, AND HIS VIZIER MUHAMMAD AMIR. THESE MEN AND THIS WOMAN ARE ON THE RUN.
THEY'RE THIEVES.
PEACE BE UPON YOU, MEN OF CÓRDOBA. YOU WON'T HAVE ANY TROUBLE WITH US.
WE ARE CONVERTED TO ISLAM. THE KING OF LISBON LETS US SAIL THE TAGUS TO CAPTURE SLAVES...
...BUT WE DON'T TAKE MUSLIMS.
THESE ARE INDEED MUSLIMS.

AH, NONONONONO! I'M NOT A MUSLIM.
I'M...
I'M JEWISH!

AND I'M A CHRISTIAN! BLESSED ARE YOU, MARY, FULL OF GRACE!

BLESS... BLESSED ARE YOU...

IF THEY'RE NOT MUSLIM, THAT'S ANOTHER STORY...

I DON'T REALLY CARE ABOUT THEM. TO TELL YOU THE TRUTH, I'M OFFERING THEM TO YOU.
ALL I ASK IS THAT YOU LET ME HAVE BACK WHAT THEY'VE STOLEN.

NEVER! THESE BOOKS AREN'T YOURS! THEY BELONG TO ALL MANKIND!

BRAVE MADJUS! YOU LOOK LIKE INTELLIGENT MEN TO ME! DON'T LET THIS DISGRACE UNFOLD!

WHAT, IS THAT WHAT THEY STOLE? OLD BOOKS?

HUH?
OH, NO. NOBODY CARES ABOUT THAT.

WHAT I WANT IS THE SWORD THERE.

WHA...? THE... THIS SWORD?

THEY DON'T WANT THE BOOKS...

WAS THIS SWORD ON THE MULE WHEN YOU STOLE IT, MARWAN?
Y... YEAH, I...
YES, THIS IS THE SWORD THEY'VE STOLEN. THE VIZIER IS VERY FOND OF IT.

I'LL LEAVE YOU THESE SLAVES AS COMPENSATION.
SOUNDS PERFECT TO ME!

LET'S GO! GIVE HIM THE SWORD!

HEY... WAIT A MINUTE!
BRING IT OVER HERE.
+VLFBERHT+
WHERE DID YOU GET THIS SWORD, JEW?

*"BLACK MAN," AMONG THE VIKINGS

HE WAS BJÖRN'S RIGHT-HAND MAN.

OVER A CENTURY AGO, WITH THIS ULFBERHT IN HIS FIST, HAREK DOG-FACE AND HIS MEN WREAKED DEATH AND DESTRUCTION ON THE STREETS OF SEVILLE FOR SEVEN DAYS.

THE WHOLE POPULATION FLED. THE CALIPH SUFFERED THE FRIGHT OF HIS LIFE.

YOU MUST KNOW THIS, RIGHT?

I ALSO KNOW THAT WE TOOK BACK THE CITY SOME TIME LATER AND EXTERMINATED THE INVADERS.
BUT TWENTY *BLÅMENN* DIED FOR EVERY DANE WHO FELL.
DON'T BE DIFFICULT. THESE SLAVES ARE VALUABLE. YOU'LL BE COMPENSATED BY SELLING THEM.
AN *ULFBERHT* HAS NOTHING TO DO WITH MONEY, *BLÅMANN.*
IF YOU WANT IT, COME AND TAKE IT.

**GOLD COINAGE OF THE TIME

HAHAHAHAHA!
IT'S A DEAL!

NOW GO, BEFORE I CHANGE MY MIND. GO AND KISS YOUR VIZIER'S BACKSIDE!

THEY... THEY DON'T WANT...

VERY GOOD! LET'S TAKE A LOOK AT WHAT I'VE WON HERE...
A HALF-DEAD MULE, A PILE OF OLD PARCHMENT, A FEVERISH OLD SAQALIBA...
WELL...
FORTUNATELY, THERE ARE TWO YOUNGSTERS HERE, AS WELL.
THE WOMAN WILL DISTRACT MY MEN...
...AND THE OTHER WILL GO TO THE GALLEYS OF SICILY.
FELLOWS! BUILD ME A BIG FIRE WITH ALL THESE OLD GRIMOIRES. TONIGHT, WE'LL EAT THE MULE AND HAVE THE GIRL DANCE. TOMORROW, WE HEAD BACK TO LISBOA. IN TWO DAYS, WE'RE OFF TO IFRIQIYA.
COME THIS WAY, YOU.
TAKE YOUR PAWS OFF ME, YOU IMBECILE!
PARDON?
ARE YOU REALLY THE LEADER OF THIS FILTHY GANG? I DON'T BELIEVE IT! I'VE NEVER SEEN ANYONE SO BAD AT BUSINESS! AND HE'S EVEN SO PROUD OF HIS STUPIDITY THAT HE'S RUBBING HIS HANDS IN GLEE ABOUT IT!
GULP. UH... LUBNA...

WHAT? WHAT?!?
WE'VE BEEN WALKING FOR DAYS! NO FOOD, NO WATER! WE'RE TRYING TO SAVE WHAT WE CAN... DID YOU SEE WHAT I SAW?
THESE MORONS ARE READY TO KILL EACH OTHER OVER A PIECE OF IRON! OH, A BIT OF IRON BETTER THAN OTHERS!
TO KILL MORE EASILY!
A SLAB OF MEAT, A FEW COINS, A WOMAN TO SHARE, AND THEY'RE HAPPY!
LOOK AT THEM!
GREAT.. BUNCH OF...
IDIOTS!
YOU'RE IN FOR A ROUGH NIGHT, KID.

THOSE ARE MY ODDS RIGHT NOW, YES...
...UNLESS YOU AND YOUR MEN SUDDENLY EXPERIENCE A SPASM OF INTELLIGENCE AND DECIDE TO BECOME ***TRULY RICH***, MUCH GREATER THAN A SMALL PURSE OF DINARS AND AN OLD LEG OF MULE!

BUT FOR THAT, YOU'D NEED A MIRACLE!

TRULY RICH? WHAT ARE YOU TALKING ABOUT? IF ANYTHING HERE HAD GREATER VALUE, THE *BLÅMENN* WOULDN'T HAVE SO EASILY ABANDONED IT.

EUH... NOBLE TRADER... THIS IS A (SOMEWHAT FRAYED) COPY...

...OF "THE BOOK OF ADDITION AND SUBTRACTION ACCORDING TO THE HINDU CALCULATION," BY AL-KHWARIZMI.

IT'S A UNIQUE BOOK, THIS SIDE OF THE SEA.
THE EMPEROR OF CONSTANTINOPLE ASKED US SEVERAL TIMES FOR A LATIN TRANSLATION, BUT WE ALWAYS LACKED THE TIME FOR IT.

HE OFFERED 3,000 DINARS FOR A COPY AT THE TIME... TODAY, IT WOULD SURELY BE MUCH MORE THAN THAT.

AND THIS DIOSCORIDES (ADMITTEDLY A LITTLE WORN OUT), HAD BAGHDAD EXTREMELY JEALOUS, BECAUSE IT'S SUBTLY ILLUSTRATED AND TRANSLATED DIRECTLY FROM THE GREEK...
...WHEREAS THE COPY IN BAGHDAD WAS TRANSLATED FROM PERSIAN INTO ARABIC, THE PERSIAN TEXT ITSELF HAVING BEEN TRANSLATED FROM GREEK...

...BUT WITH A LOT OF LITTLE APPROXIMATIONS IN THE PLANT NAMES.

HERE, TAKE A LOOK...
DO YOU FOLLOW?
UH...

IT'S WORTH AT LEAST 5,000 GOLD DINARS.
FIVE THOU--!!
TELL HIM ABOUT "THE BOOK OF SONGS."

AH, YES!

THIS IS THE VERY FIRST (ALBEIT SLIGHTLY CREASED) EDITION OF "THE BOOK OF SONGS," THE MOST COMPLETE ANTHOLOGY OF ARABIC SONGS AND POEMS, COMPILED BY ABU AL-FARAJ.
FIFTY YEARS OF WORK.

THE CALIPH AL-HAKAM II SENT A THOUSAND GOLD DINARS IN ADVANCE, FROM CÓRDOBA TO BAGHDAD, TO ASSURE HE'D RECEIVE THIS WORK WHEN IT WAS COMPLETED.

TODAY, IT'S WORTH TEN TIMES AS MUCH. IT'S THE VERY FIRST!

AS FOR IBN FIRNAS' "TREATISE OF MECHANICS," WELL... THEN WE'RE REALLY APPROACHING THE SUBLIME! IMAGINE THE DETAILING OF ARTIFICIAL WINGS...

AND THEN THERE'S RAZI!

AND "THE BOOK OF ANIMALS" BY AL-JAHIZ, AS WELL...
AND THEN...

ENOUGH.
ENOUGH!

DO YOU... HAVE MANY MORE OF THESE?
I'D SAY... CLOSE TO A HUNDRED.
HUH?! AND THE SOLDIERS JUST LEFT IT HERE?
SOLDIERS ARE THE SAME EVERYWHERE. THEY DON'T KNOW WHAT'S VALUABLE.

THE VIZIER HIMSELF HAS JUST BURNED A FEW HUNDRED... A FEW *THOUSAND* BOOKS. IN CÓRDOBA.

WHA... WHAT? BUT WHY?
UH... WELL, THAT'S... EUH...
TO SIMPLIFY.

SIMPLIFY? SIMPLIFY WHAT?
THE...SOLDIERS' LIVES.
HUH?

NATURALLY, THE BINDINGS HAVE TO BE REDONE AND REPAIRED...
WE KNOW HOW TO DO THAT. IT'S WHAT WE DO.
AND THIS MAN HAS ALL THE CONTACTS! IN BAGHDAD, CONSTANTINOPLE, ALEXANDRIA, ROME. HE OFTEN CORRESPONDS WITH OTHER PROMINENT ARCHIVISTS...

HIM?

YOU HAVE TO TAKE CARE OF HIM IN THE MEANTIME. WITHOUT HIM, IT'S ALL WORTHLESS. WE'RE JUST HIS ASSISTANTS.

CHIEF, WHEN'S THE GIRL GONNA DANCE?

YOU'RE THE ONE WHO'LL HAVE TO DANCE AROUND THE FIRE IF YOU TOUCH A HAIR ON THEIR HEADS, YOU IDIOT!

RODDICK! WHERE ARE YOU, YOU OLD BARREL?
I... I'M HERE, CHIEF.

USE YOUR SCIENCE. IF HE DIES, YOU DIE.
GULP. O...OH?

CHANGE OF PLANS! LET'S GET ON BOARD AND GET GOING! JUST IN CASE THE VIZIER'S MEN CHANGE THEIR MINDS.
TO THE BOATS!
AH? AND... WHAT ABOUT THE MULE?

WE CUT IT UP AND STORE IT WITH THE FOOD SUPPLY.
NO!
YOU HAVE NO IDEA WHAT THAT MULE'S BEEN THROUGH! THE TRIP SHE'S TAKEN IS FAR GREATER THAN YOUR LITTLE BOAT TRIPS!

UH... I'M NOT SURE ABOUT THAT...

BUT SHE'S HALF-DEAD ALREADY.
OH, NO. WHAT CAN WE DO?

NOT MUCH, EXCEPT PUT HER OUT OF HER MISERY.
NO!

WE'VE GOT TO SAVE HER! SHE'S... SHE'S WORTH THE MOST MONEY!
WHAT?!
MUCH MORE THAN THE BOOKS! THIS ISN'T JUST ANY MULE. IT'S... IT'S A KNOWLEDGEABLE MULE.
ARE YOU KIDDING ME?
NOT AT ALL! WE'VE RAISED HER FROM AN EARLY AGE, STIMULATING HER MIND...
WE INTRODUCED HER TO ASTRONOMY, PHILOSOPHY...
A CLEVER MULE?
SHE KNOWS EVERYTHING! IF SHE WERE IN BETTER SHAPE, SHE'D SHOW OFF HER TALENTS! SHE'LL EASILY GET YOU 10,000 DINARS IN CONSTANTINOPLE.
YOU... YOU SWEAR YOU'RE TELLING THE TRUTH?
I SWEAR IT!
BEFORE ALMIGHTY GOD, WHO SEES ALL AND KNOWS ALL?
...GULP... I...
I'LL DO EVEN BETTER THAN THAT. I'LL PROVE IT TO YOU.

CAN YOU LAY OUT
THE MANUSCRIPTS
YOU'RE HOLDING
BEFORE HER?

OH, WISE MULE,
CAN YOU TELL US WHO
YOU THINK IS THE GREATEST
MATHEMATICIAN IN THE
WORLD?

WOOOP!
THANK YOU. LET'S
SEE WHICH AUTHOR
YOU SUGGEST.

DO
YOU READ
ARABIC?
NO, BUT
RODDICK READS
A LITTLE...

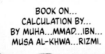

BOOK ON...
CALCULATION BY...
BY MUHA...MMAD...IBN...
MUSA AL-KHWA...RIZMI.
NATURALLY,
IT'S AL-KHWARIZMI!
HAHAHA! SHE KNOWS
EVERYTHING,
I TELL YOU!

SEEMS
SO...

LOAD THE MULE!
WHAT DOES THIS MULE HAVE AGAINST AL-KHWARIZMI?

COME ON. WE'RE ALIVE.
UNTIL THEY FIND OUT YOU LIED ABOUT THE MULE.

LET'S HAVE CONFI-DENCE IN THE FUTURE.

LET'S GO! HIGH SPIRITS, MEN! SET A COURSE FOR THE MEDITERRANEAN! WE'RE GONNA BE RICH!

YOU KNOW THE SECRETS OF BOOKS, AND I KNOW BUSINESS.
YOU DIDN'T EXACTLY DAZZLE US WITH YOUR BUSINESS ACUMEN EARLIER.

IS THAT SO?

YOU TRADED A MYTHICAL SWORD, PROBABLY WORTH A FORTUNE, FOR THREE SLAVES AND A FEW GOLD COINS.
THAT'S A PRETTY SO-SO DEAL, DON'T YOU THINK?
IT WAS JUST A COPY.

I TOLD YOU, *ULFBERHT* ARE VERY RARE. MOST OF THEM OUT IN THE WORLD ARE COUNTERFEITS.
I KNOW HOW TO SPOT THEM.

ON THAT ONE, THE CROSSES WERE IN THE WRONG PLACE.

YOUR VIZIER PAID GOOD MONEY FOR A COPY OF AN *ULFBERHT*. IN REALITY, IT'S JUST A PLAIN OL' SWORD.
BUT HAGGLING IS PART OF THE FUN OF TRADING, ISN'T IT? HA HA!

HAHAHAHAHA!

WHATEVER SWORD MUHAMMAD AMIR HELD IN HIS HANDS THAT YEAR...

...IT GAVE HIM THE CONFIDENCE HE NEEDED TO LAUNCH AN ASSAULT ON THE CHRISTIAN KINGDOMS.

HE, ONCE A ZEALOUS ADMINISTRATOR, BECAME OVERNIGHT THE TERRIBLE ALMANZOR, THE VICTORIOUS, WHO SPENT HIS LIFE ON THE BATTLEFIELDS.

FROM 977 UNTIL HIS
DEATH IN 1002, HE
UNDERTOOK MORE THA
50 MILITARY CAMPAIG
THAT FRAGMENTED TH
CALIPHATE AND EVENTUA
LED TO ITS DOWNFALL

IT IS SAID THAT, AFTER E
BATTLE, HE COLLECTED
DUST THAT COVERED HIM
THAT HE MIGHT BE BUR
WITH IT UPON HIS DEAT

AND SO IT WAS.

AFTER THE REIGN OF ALMANZOR, THE CALIPHATE OF CÓRDOBA BROKE INTO A CONSTELLATION OF SMALL, CORRUPT, AND AGGRESSIVE FIEFDOMS: THE TAIFAS.

WITH LITTLE INTEREST IN CONQUEST, THE LORDS OF THE TAIFAS RELIED ON CHRISTIAN AND BERBER MERCENARIES TO WAGE WAR.

THEIR TRUE RIVALRY WAS IN THE ARTS AND SCIENCES.

IN THEIR OWN WAY, THEY RETURNED LIFE TO THE CULTURAL VITALITY SEEN IN THE BEGINNINGS OF AL-ANDALUS.

ECHOING THE MYSTERIOUS DESTRUCTION OF THE GREAT LIBRARY OF ALEXANDRIA...

...THE DESTRUCTION OF THE LIBRARY OF CÓRDOBA WAS AN IRREPARABLE LOSS FOR HUMAN KNOWLEDGE.
IT HERALDED A DISASTROUS SERIES OF EVENTS.

IN 1239, POPE GREGORY IX ORDERED THE KINGS OF FRANCE, SPAIN, AND ENGLAND TO CONFISCATE ALL COPIES OF THE TALMUD.

IN 1242, LOUIS IX BURNED FOUR CARTLOADS OF THE TALMUD IN THE PLACE DE GRÈVE.

IN 1258, BAGHDAD WAS TAKEN BY HULAGU KHAN, GRANDSON OF GENGHIS KHAN, AND ALL THE BOOK IN THE BAGHDAD LIBRARY WERE DELIBERATELY THROWN INTO THE TIGRIS

IT IS SAID THAT THE INK MINGLED WITH THE BLOOD OF THE 500,000 DEAD IN THE RIVER'S WATERS.

THEN IT WAS THE QURAN'S TURN TO BE BURNED DURING THE RECONQUISTA IN SPAIN.

IN 1499, FRANCISCO JIMÉNEZ DE CISNEROS, ARCHBISHOP OF TOLEDO, HAD THOUSANDS OF ARABIC BOOKS PUBLICLY BURNED IN GRANADA. PERHAPS SOME OF THEM CONTAINED ANNOTATIONS WRITTEN IN THE HAND OF AL-HAKAM II OR ABD AL-RAHMAN III?

AT THE SAME TIME, IN MEXICO, FATHER ZUMÁRRAGA AND BISHOP LANDA COLLECTED AND THEN BURNED ALL THE MAYAN CODICES AND DOCUMENTS, BECAUSE THEY WERE...

..."SUPERSTITIONS AND DEMONIC LIES."

ONLY FOUR OR FIVE CODICES ESCAPED THE MASSACRE.

WE'LL NEVER KNOW MUCH MORE ABOUT PRE-COLUMBIAN MAYAN CULTURE.

AND YET, DESPITE THE DESTRUCTION, DESPITE THE RECURRENT, CULTURAL "GENOCIDE," KNOWLEDGE SOMETIMES FOUND ITS OWN WAY.

IT WAS THROUGH ARABIC TRANSLATIONS THAT EUROPE DISCOVERED GREEK PHILOSOPHY, MATHEMATICS, AND INDIAN STORIES.

JEAN DE LA FONTAINE DISCOVERED, THANKS TO BIDPAI, ARABIC VERSIONS OF INDIAN TALES TAKEN FROM AESOP, WHO HIMSELF HAD REPRISED THEM FROM EVEN OLDER, PERSIAN TALES.

AL-KHWARIZMI GAVE HIS NAME TO THE ALGORITHM AND ALGEBRA.

DE VINCI'S "FLYING MACHINES" LOOK STRANGELY LIKE THOSE OF IBN FIRNAS.

DA VINCI PUT A TAIL ON HIS PROTOTYPE....

...BUT HE NEVER TESTED IT HIMSELF.

AL-JAHIZ, IN HIS "BOOK OF ANIMALS," REFERS TO THE SNAKE AS AN "EEL THAT HAS ADAPTED TO LIFE OUT OF WATER"...

...A THOUSAND YEARS BEFORE CHARLES DARWIN...

...WHO PROBABLY KNEW NOTHING ABOUT IT.

OF THE 600 PAGES OF THE ORIGINAL MANUSCRIPT FOR DARWIN'S "ORIGIN OF SPECIES," ONLY 45 HAVE REACHED US. DARWIN HIMSELF KEPT THE REST BECAUSE HIS CHILDREN DREW ON THEM...

...JUST AS TARID DID ON AL-JAHIZ'S "BOOK OF ANIMALS."

TARID NEVER DARED REVEAL TO MARWAN THAT AL-JAHIZ THE GLOBULAR HAD SUFFOCATED TO DEATH UNDER HIS OWN FALLEN BOOKCASE...

AFTER THE POPULARIZATION OF THE PRINTING PRESS, THE DESTRUCTION OF BOOKS BECAME MORE SYMBOLIC THAN EFFECTIVE, BUT IT DID NOT STOP.

YESTERDAY: THE VATICAN, HITLER, STALIN, MAO...

TODAY: ISIL, BOKO HARAM...

AND, IN ALL ERAS, THE ZEALOTS OF ALL CHURCHES, AS SOON AS THE OPPORTUNITY ARISES.

IN 2007, THE BAGHDAD LIBRARY WAS AGAIN COMPLETELY DESTROYED, THIS TIME BY AMERICAN BOMBING CAMPAIGNS.

OOPS...

SORRY, GUYS!

OF THE 400,000 BOOKS IN THE CALIPHS' LIBRARY, ONLY ONE WAS EVER FOUND. IN 1936, IN FEZ, MOROCCO.

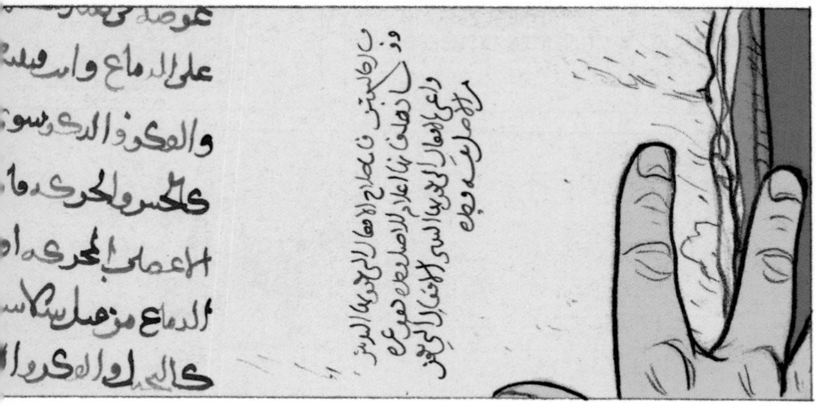

IT BORE THE ANNOTATIONS OF AL-HAKAM II.

AND TOMORROW?
?!
THE NEXT PERIL TO
THREATEN KNOWLEDGE...

ACCESS DENIED

FIN
LUPANO-CHEMINEAU
2021

AFTERWORD

The Library Mule of Córdoba is set in the Caliphate of Córdoba at the end of the 10th century, a time that is considered the political and cultural apogee of al-Andalus, the name given to the part of the Iberian Peninsula conquered at the beginning of the 8th century by the troops of the Umayyad Caliphate in Damascus (Syria).

The Caliphate of Córdoba

It was in 929 that the reigning prince of al-Andalus, Abd al-Rahman III (r. 912-961), had himself proclaimed Caliph. His ancestors had not dared to claim this title and had contented themselves, since 756, with the title of Emir. The difference between the two titles—Emir and Caliph—is very important.

When Muhammad, the prophet of Islam, died in 632, he had no sons to inherit his power, only daughters. The Muslims elected one of his companions to lead the fledgling community. Then, after some trial and error, which resulted in the testing of different systems of designation of the Khalifa (lit. "successor [of the prophet]" or "lieutenant [of God on Earth]")—consensus, co-optation, will, election by a restricted council—a ruler, Mu'awiya (r. 661-680), was appointed in 661, who established a dynastic system by having his own son succeed him during his lifetime. He took Damascus in Syria as his capital, where he had been governor for about twenty years. This was the birth of the Umayyad Dynasty of Damascus (661-750).

This monopolization of the Caliphal function by the Umayyad family was not without opposition among the first faithful and members of the Prophet's family who felt excluded, in particular Ali, the Prophet's cousin, who became his son-in-law by marrying Fatima. Ali is thus the father of grandsons of the Prophet. The followers of Ali, removed from power by the Umayyads, were at the origin of Shi'ism, the "party of Ali," and considered him to be the first Imam ("guide") of the community—i.e. the legitimate ruler—his sons and Fatima being the second and third Imams respectively.

In 750, the Umayyads of Damascus were overthrown by a mass revolt, supported not only by the Shiites but also by non-Arab converts (mainly Persian), who were removed from power by the Umayyads who systematically favored the Arabs in the allocation of positions of responsibility and in the distribution of funds.

It was the Abbasids, descendants of an uncle of the prophet, al-Abbas (d. 653), who seized power, founding Baghdad and massacring all the members of the Umayyad dynasty at a banquet of "reconciliation." Legend has it that Abd al-Rahman I (r. 756-788), whose mother was Berber, managed to escape the massacre by swimming across the Tigris, taking refuge in Córdoba where he founded the Umayyad Emirate of Córdoba by ousting the Abbasid governor appointed by Baghdad in 756.

For nearly two centuries, the Principality of Córdoba claimed to be the continuation of the Caliphate of Damascus, but its leaders did not dare to claim the title of Caliph that had been wrested from them in 750, because there could only be one Caliph.

Located on the western periphery of the Muslim world at the time, the Umayyad Principality of Córdoba was then the conservatory of Syrian practices: the armies carried the white banners of the Umayyads of Damascus against the black banners of the Abbasids, they bore the names of the cities of Syria-Palestine—armies of Homs, Palestine, the Jordan River, etc.—the Andalusian mosques were oriented towards the south-southeast, as in Syria, and not east-southeast as they should be so that the faithful pray in the direction of Mecca...

From a geopolitical point of view, the opposition to the Abbasids in Baghdad also had important consequences: it explains, in particular, why the Umayyads of Córdoba turned their gaze towards Constantinople and the Byzantine Empire, according to the principle of "the enemies of my enemies are my friends." The work in the Great Mosque of Córdoba, mentioned in *The Library Mule of Córdoba,* called on Byzantine craftsmen for the mosaics of the Mihrab—the niche (theoretically) indicating the direction of Mecca on the qibla wall in the prayer hall.

The use of mosaic decoration, rare in the Islamic world, was intended to recall the mosaics of the Great Mosque of Damascus, designed at the end of the 7th century by Byzantine craftsmen.

For nearly two centuries, the Umayyad Emirs of Córdoba challenged the power of the Abbasids. Still, they did not dare to claim for themselves the title of Caliph. It was not until the beginning of the 10th century and the reign of Abd al-Rahman III that the rulers of al-Andalus took the plunge. It must be said that in 909, a Shiite revolt took place in Ifriqiya (present-day Tunisia), and a Shiite Fatimid Imamate-Caliphate, mentioned in *The Library Mule of Córdoba* and taking its name from Fatima, the daughter of the prophet, was proclaimed in Kairouan. This new power broke the unity of the Caliph and opposed both the Abbasid Caliphal dynasty of Baghdad and the Emiral dynasty of the Umayyads of Córdoba.

In 969, the Fatimids, for whom power was in the East, transferred their seat to Egypt, where they founded a new capital, al-Qahira ("the Victorious," Cairo), definitively abandoning Maghreb and moving with them the tombs of the first sovereigns of the dynasty.

Until 969, therefore, the Umayyads of Córdoba faced the Fatimids in western Maghreb (present-day Algeria and Morocco) through Berber tribes. This explains the very close ties forged by the Caliphs of Córdoba with the populations of Maghreb: exchanges of gifts, embassies, alliances. The somewhat dark picture painted by *The Library Mule of Córdoba* of the Berber "mercenaries" called into al-Andalus by the Vizier Ibn Abi Amir al-Mansur takes up the partisan bias of an "Arab" historiography that has condemned the inhabitants of Maghreb to shame since the conquest of the 7th century because of the numerous Berber revolts that targeted the new Arab powers. The last of these revolts was that of the Berber tribe of the Kutama, who brought the Fatimids to power in Ifriqiya in 909.

If the Umayyad Caliphs of Córdoba were politically opposed to the Abbasid caliphs of Baghdad, and if they distinguished themselves by valuing their Arabness in relation to the Persian influence that prevailed at the Baghdad court, they were inversely inspired by them from a cultural, ceremonial, musical, and sartorial point of view. *The Library Mule of Córdoba* thus evokes the ordering and purchasing of books, sometimes paid for with several thousand gold coins (dinars). That said, it does not seem that Córdoba was a great center of translation from Greek into Arabic. It was in Baghdad, on the initiative of several enlightened Caliphs, that works of medicine, philosophy, astronomy, mathematics, and geography were translated by Christians, Jews, and converts, either from Greek or Persian. The role of the Persians was also very important at the court of Baghdad—as recalled, in *The Library Mule,* by the recurring motif of the treatise (appetizing for the mule) of Al-Khwarizmi, a Persian mathematician, astronomer, and geographer, who died in 850. There are other indications of the influence of the Abbasid court on Córdoba: during the beginnings of Islam, the Caliphs lived simply, but this began to change with the Umayyad caliphs of Damascus, who had superb palaces built in the Syrian steppe. However, it was in Baghdad that, under Persian influence, a real ceremonial culture was set up around the Caliphs. One person in particular had a very great influence, according to the sources: Ziryab, a Kurdish-Persian born in 789 near Mosul (present-day Iraq) and who died in Córdoba in 857. He is said to have introduced oriental dishes, the lute, and Iraqi musical traditions to Córdoba.

From a political point of view, it was in the East that the character of the Vizier, the bête noire of the Caliph, appeared. The fate of a dynasty of Persian Viziers, the Barmakids, in the service of the famous Harun al-Rashid (r. 786-809) and his sons, became a literary motif in the tales of the *Arabian Nights*, which depict the tormented relations between these Viziers and their masters. The very art of *The Library Mule* harnesses the influence of Orientalism, the tales of the *Thousand and One Nights*, current events, and the famous collaborative work of René Goscinny and Jean Tabary, as well as the film based on it, *Iznogoud*, about an evil Vizier who wants to "become Caliph in the place of the good Caliph," Haroun El Poussah: The "Iranian-style" turban of the Ulema, the Machiavellian profile of the famous chamberlain Ibn Abi Amir al-Mansur (r. 978-1002), whose reign actually corresponds to the political apogee of the Umayyad Caliphate of Córdoba. *The Library Mule* thus evokes a very real episode of religious rigidity at the end of the 10th century in Córdoba, an episode that refers to the very special relationship between people of knowledge in Islam and the political powers.

Knowledge and Power in Islam and Córdoba

In 751, the Battle of Talas, on the border with China, took place between the Abbasid armies and the armies of the Chinese general Xuanzong, emperor of the Tang dynasty. The Abbasid victory led to the conquest of a large trove and the capture of many prisoners, including paper artisans. The significance of this event has often been underestimated.

With the secret of papermaking, the concept of writing in abundance and cheaply entered the Islamic world, which profoundly disrupted society, culture, and civilization. While at the same time and for several centuries to come, the Christian kingdoms and Byzantines wrote little because the manufacturing of the writing medium, parchment, was extremely expensive—it was calf, lamb, or goat skins—the written word spread massively in the Muslim world, from China to the Iberian Peninsula. This technical knowledge allowed the transfer of all ancient Greek, Latin, and Persian knowledge to the Muslim provinces. A veritable culture of writing then spread, along with the habit of copying books, commenting on them, and annotating them in the margins (as mentioned in *The Library Mule*).

This is also reflected in the religious world: scholars (Ulema) copy the text of the Qur'an, and the traditions (Hadiths) attributed to the Prophet, write commentaries on it, and then make commentaries on commentaries; this is called exegesis. They did the same with works translated from Greek into Arabic (mathematics, algebra, astronomy, astrology, philosophy, alchemy, medicine, Aristotle's Letter to Alexander, The Book of Animals by al-Jāhiz), or from Persian into Arabic (Kalīla wa Dimna...).

This transfer of ancient knowledge was commissioned by the Abbasid rulers of Baghdad in the 9th century, and it nourished the learned world in all the territories of Islam. The discovery of Aristotle, Plato, Plotinus... and, generally speaking, all the ancient philosophers had a very great influence on Muslim theology and gave rise to much debate among scholars. The question arose very early on of the reconciliation of the truths drawn from Reason with those derived from Revelation. In the 9th century, the Abbasid caliphs actively participated in these debates by attempting to establish themselves as the only authorized interpreters of the Qur'anic text. This resulted in the imprisonment or torture of several scholars who refused to submit to Caliphal authority with regard to religious dogma.

This competition over the interpretation of the dogma of Islam between political powers and the guild of scholars continues to this day. It is less a fusion of the political and the religious than a competition between two systems of authority: the one drawn from reading and reflection, the one inherited from the exercise of power. Sovereigns were forced to call on scholars for their administration: accounting, drafting official letters, legitimizing their power, while scholars needed rulers, who financed their activities as patrons. In Islam, mastery of literature thus opened the doors to power, but this association was strewn with pitfalls and many scholars paid with their lives for being too close to those in power.

In Córdoba, the first Caliphs revived the great Abbasid tradition of patronage with the creation of the largest library in the West and the accumulation of books purchased from all over the Muslim world. Translations from Greek into Arabic took place mainly in the East, in Baghdad, although some are attested in Córdoba. It is therefore mainly works in Arabic that constitute the collection of royal or private libraries. It is not clear what happened to the famous library of the Caliphs of Córdoba. It is likely that these books were dispersed according to the vagaries of politics (conquests and reconquests). It had several hundred thousand books, while the scriptoria of the monasteries of the Latin world possessed only a few dozen, or at best a few hundred (due to the cost of parchment).

It is difficult to know whether the book burning at the heart of the plot of *The Library Mule* took place, or if it really took place on this scale. It is indeed mentioned in some sources of the 11th century, most often nostalgic for the Caliphate and its greatness, and they claim that it lasted 6 days. If it is difficult for today's historian to confirm or deny this event, it is for several reasons: first, the small number of textual sources; second, the lack of archaeological confirmation; and, finally, the importance that books and libraries continue to play during the next two centuries in al-Andalus and the Maghreb. It must be said that the low cost of making paper allowed for the multiplication of copies. As a result, there were few one-of-a-kind examples. Moreover, when the chronicles of the time mention such episodes, they are usually limited to certain authors or currents of thought. Paradoxically, it was not so much works of philosophy, clearly identified as "outside" Islam, even if they profoundly influenced it, than works of Muslim mysticism that were targeted. Thus, the followers of the scholar Ibn Masarra, mentioned in *The Library Mule*, were persecuted because their particular philosophical and mystical conceptions of Islam threatened the traditional religious authorities.

The period of the reign of Ibn Abî 'Amîr al-Mansur, whom Andalusian sources more often call Hâdjib—that is, chamberlain or mayor of the palace—rather than Vizier, was indeed a time of religious stiffening. This character is a civilian and a scholar working in the tax administration. The support that Subh (Aurora), the wife of the Caliph al-Hakam II, mother of the young Hisham II, gave him during his career was open to all kinds of speculation. In order to impose himself at court and gain acceptance from the population, the man known in Latin sources as Almanzor decided to rely on the clerics (the better to hide the fact that he exercised power in place of the legitimate sovereign) and to use military jihad against the Christian kingdoms in the north of the Peninsula. During his 26-year reign, he led 52 expeditions, two a year, which led him to capture Barcelona in 985 and, in 997, Santiago de Compostela, where he brought the bells of the cathedral back to Córdoba. At the same time, he cultivated his network of alliances by marrying a daughter of each of the Christian kings of Navarre, León, and Castile. One of the sons of these unions, Sandjûl (Sanchuelo, "Little Sancho," grandson of the King of Navarre), wanted, unlike his much more prudent father, to actually become Caliph in place of the current Caliph.

He was executed in 1009 by the people of Córdoba for this sacrilege.

Women and Slaves in the 10th Century in Western Islam

Two of the main protagonists of *The Library Mule of Córdoba* are slaves: a eunuch (Tarid, the librarian) and a copyist (Lubna); other slaves appear in secondary roles, and sometimes in positions of authority, such as Subh (Aurora), the widow of the caliph al-Hakam II, a close supporter of the chamberlain Ibn Abî 'Âmir al-Mansur. It may come as a surprise in a slave society to see slaves in positions of power. Yet this is one of the characteristics of slavery in the medieval Muslim world.

Indeed, there are several types of slaves. The first, the one about which we have the least information, is that of the "common" slaves: they are assigned to domestic chores, to work in the fields or to the rigors of handicrafts, and therefore leave few traces in written sources that are mainly interested in the circles of power. The second type, which appears marginally in *The Library Mule*, but which is of great importance in Islam, concerns the army. Military slaves are known in the East as Mamluk. In Egypt, in the 13th century, the Mamluks founded an empire that lasted two centuries until the Ottoman conquest. Literally, Mamluk means "possessed", "belonging [to someone]." In al-Andalus, this system of Mamluk takes a specific form, that of the Saqaliba, the "sclavonians." From the Slavic world, young children were captured and trained in the profession of arms. *The Library Mule of Córdoba* recalls the trajectory of these slaves captured in Eastern Europe, and some of whom, brought to Verdun, were castrated there, then sent to al-Andalus where they were sold, such as the librarian Tarid. Nevertheless, these slaves were intended mainly for the profession of arms and they formed the praetorian guards of the governors, Emirs, or Caliphs of the region. In some provinces, they gained positions of strength and prestige, and even managed to seize power at the time of the crisis of the Caliphate of Córdoba in 1031, founding independent principalities that they ruled, though they were originally slaves. Unable to have children, they were naturally unable to found any dynasties, which contributed to the political instability of the regions they ruled.

The third type of slaves was that of specialized slaves: especially women (jawârî), dancers, musicians, copyists (such as Lubna), wives or concubines for the Caliph's harem (such as Subh/Aurora), but also men such as Tarid the librarian... Again, it should be noted that, unlike in the Latin world of the time, the son of a slave could claim to inherit the power of his Caliph father. Lubna's destiny is peculiar: her biography has been preserved in several biobibliographical dictionaries of scholars from the eleventh and thirteenth centuries, which describe her as a grammarian, poet, mathematician, and, above all, as a talented calligrapher. This quality is said to have been spotted while she was employed, like many of her peers, as secretary of the Caliph's chancery. She is said to have worked in Madînat al-Zahrâ'—the palatial city mentioned in *The Library Mule of Córdoba* and built by 'Abd al-Rahmân III (r. 912-961)—in close collaboration with another slave, also a secretary, who acquired a great knowledge of astronomy and was an expert in the handling of the astrolabe.

These different enslaved characters, who structure the story of *The Library Mule of Córdoba*, in fact reveal a social organization, power relations, and a specificity of slavery in the land of Islam which contrasts with the image that we can have of slavery today in an anachronistic way.

Conclusion

At the beginning of the eleventh century, the Caliphate of Córdoba sank into a very serious political crisis that is evoked in *The Library Mule*. However, this breakup of the central state of Córdoba in 1031 into some thirty independent principalities, which received the name of Taifas (from Arabic, tâ'ifa in the singular, tawâ'if in the plural, i.e. "parties"), did not result in a cultural, literary, poetic, philosophical, or artistic decline.

In fact, quite the opposite is true. Each of these Taifas aspired to be a new Córdoba in order to inherit its prestige. To this end, each little ruler attracted poets and scholars to his court. Bruna Soravia, a historian specializing in this period, has described the Taifas' poets as kingmakers because of the power they derived from the verses they composed. By their praises or their satires, they could make or break the kings who snatched them up at a high price. The 11th century in Andalusia was the century of an efflorescence of scientific, literary, poetic, philosophical, and religious knowledge. The time of the Hajib Ibn Abi 'Āmir al-Mansur can be considered a political apogee for the Caliphate of Córdoba: it dominated the entire Muslim West through its influence in the Maghreb, and it inspired terror in the Christian kingdoms of the north of the Iberian Peninsula. The period of the Taifas, in comparison, was one of a major political crisis, marked by a military weakening due to internal competitions between the various rival principalities, lavish expenditures incurred to create brilliant courts (to the great displeasure of subjects dissatisfied with the increase in taxes), and the correlative strengthening of the Christian kingdoms in the north of the Iberian Peninsula which managed to seize a major Muslim city, Toledo, in 1085.

Faced with the growing expansionism of the various Christian kingdoms, the impetus for al-Andalus came precisely from the Berber tribes of the Maghreb. The Almoravid Dynasty, supported by the Sanhaja tribes, founded Marrakech in 1071 and unified al-Andalus under its rule from 1086. The Almoravid Emirs relied on the jurists (fuqahâ') of the Maliki school that had dominated the Maghreb and al-Andalus since the 9th century. They gained the support of the population by reinstating Qur'anic taxation and waging military jihad against the Christian kingdoms in the north. Their reign was characterized by the rise of Sufism and mystical writings, which multiplied in reaction to the rigorist leadership of the Almoravid governors. The dynasty was overthrown in the middle of the twelfth centuryby a new reform movement, this time led by the Masmuda Berber tribes of the Atlas Mountains, who founded the largest Berber Maghreb empire that had ever existed, from Tripolitania to the Atlantic and the Iberian Peninsula. The period of Almohad rule was characterized by the flourishing of philosophy and philosophers, the first advisors and viziers of the Almohad Caliphs. The Maliki legal school was banned in favor of the Almohad interpretation of Islamic law, and the political system put in place was very original: Averroes (d. 1199), "the great Commentator" on Aristotle, whose work was to profoundly influence the Latin West, was then the closest advisor to the sovereigns, the one who would formalize the Almohad dogma.

This Almohad Caliphate, of which Marrakech was, as for the Almoravids, the Maghreb capital, was fully in line with the Umayyad Caliphate of Córdoba, of which he claimed authorship, even if he chose Seville as the regional capital in al-Andalus rather than Córdoba. The great minarets of Seville, Tlemcen, and Marrakech date from this period. One might think that this is a cultural climax followed by an era of obscurantism, but this is, again, a magnifying glass effect. Although libraries are regularly attacked, they do not disappear, they only change owners.

Pascal Buresi
Director of Research at the CNRS (UMR 5648-CIHAM, Lyon)
Director of Studies at EHESS
Scientific coordinator of the European project ITN-MIDA
(Mediating Islam in the Digital Age)